CONTENTS

1 Catholic Tradition & the Modern State   1

2 The Passing of Industrialism   17

3 The Evolution of the Modern City   39

4 Progress and Decay in Ancient and Modern Civilisations   55

5 Catholicism and Economics   75

6 Christianity and the Idea of Progress   125

7 The Crisis of the West   151

The Church & the Rise and Fall of Modernity

Dawson's Lost Essays

A collection of the early essays by

Christopher Dawson

Edited by
Mikael Thompson de Grisvaldi

Published by
Marchese di Carabàs

Copyright © 2025 Mikael Thompson de Grisvaldi.
All rights reserved.

ISBN: 978-1-7356578-7-5

1

THE CATHOLIC TRADITION AND THE MODERN STATE

THE changes that have come over Europe in the last century are too great to be ignored by anyone, but their very greatness and nearness to us prevent their being really understood. They have been admired blindly and enthusiastically as the dawn of a humanitarian millennium or they have been condemned by the traditionalists for undermining authority and order. By both parties, however, the fundamental characteristic of the new age has been misconceived. It is not liberty, but *power* which is the true note of our modern civilisation. Man has gained infinitely in his control over Nature, but he has lost the control over his own individual life. This may seem a paradox in face of the claims of an age which prides itself above everything on its democracy and liberalism, but the latter really mean only the substitution of a new ideal of social obligation for the old principles of authority and divine right. The executive has perhaps lost much of the arbitrary power that it possessed under the old *régime,* but there is no lightening of the pressure exercised by society as a whole on the individual.

The present war must make clear to everybody the enormous increase of power in the modern State – power not only in the matter of material resources, but also in the complete subordination of the individual to the society.

Under the old *régime* however much people suffered from their rulers they kept a power over their own lives which is unknown to-day. The peasant who was tired of being robbed could take service as a hired soldier, the soldier who was dissatisfied with his life could become a religious like St. John of God or St. Ignatius, the noble who was in trouble in his own country could betake himself to the service of another prince; for the nations of Europe were then only provinces of a single great fatherland, Christendom. In the modern State, on the contrary, every man has his allotted place, and when society needs it he must give his life in its service. An official touches the handle of a great machine, and from every corner of an empire millions of men move automatically, with an utter suppression of their own individualities, to the fulfilment of one gigantic task – a task that will bring wounds and death to millions, suffering and privation to all. That is the spectacle we see to-day, in Germany above all, and more imperfectly in the other belligerent countries, and it shows us the real meaning of the changes in Europe as nothing else could do; for it is the direct result both moral and material of the last 100 years of European national organisation and progress. While men were talking of democracy and liberty, there has grown up a vast secular power like nothing that has existed since the Roman Empire. That power is the modern State. It has an influence over men's souls that formerly only religion possessed, and its claims are almost unlimited. Is it possible to think that this power is a legitimate development of the old Christian polity, or is it, as some say, unchristian in principle and a consequence of the apostasy of the modern world? Are Catholics to look on it as a possible friend and ally, or as a persecutor and an enemy?

Let us attempt to answer these questions by tracing back the new order of things to its origins and trying to discover what has been the Christian society of the past.

When the Catholic Church first came into contact with the society of the ancient world, there ensued a great struggle between the religion and the society, which lasted from 300 to 400 years. At first the Church had to live a hidden and "recollected" life. Persecution was not strong enough to crush her, rather by isolating her it preserved her from the great danger of being assimilated by the apparently all-powerful organism of the Roman Empire. Finally the Church was victorious and Christianity become the religion of the State. There follows a period in which all social institutions are recast according to the new faith and rule of life, and on the ruins of the old world a new Christian civilisation is built up. This was the civilisation of the Middle Ages, which has been so variously appraised. Its admirers have so fully realised its embodiment of Christian ideals that they have been apt to hold it up as the one Christian civilisation to which all others must approximate. It critics have attacked indiscriminately its ideals and its failures to realise them. Some Catholics, like Newman, will attack it on the latter ground, but more often it has been blamed because the critic has a conception of Christianity at variance with the Catholic conception of life that the Middle Ages strove to embody, in however faulty and temporary a shape. To value the Middle Ages justly one must realise that theirs was an immature and youthful civilisation which never reached a complete development, for the modern world belongs to a different tradition and has progressed by a series of revolts against the mediæval tradition. The Middle Ages give us, as it were, a rough sketch of what Christian society might be, but it did not live long enough to realise it.

THE NEW ORDER

Social change may proceed from two causes: (1) Religious – From a change in the social ideal and conception of life. (2) Economic – From a change in the conditions of life. A primitive people may change radically by becoming Christian; it may also change by becoming an agricultural community instead of a tribe of hunters.

Now, the changes on which modern society is founded are of both kinds. First, there were the economic and political changes of the 15th and 16th centuries that had been preparing for hundreds of years. The rise of strong national monarchies was the centre and summing up of these. Secondly, there was the discovery of the New World. Thirdly, the recovery of the learning and art of the ancient world and the advance of the science of Nature.

The result was an age of expansion and self-consciousness. Man felt himself to be of age, and gloried in the hitherto unrealised possibilities of his powers and knowledge. He grew impatient of restraint, irreverent towards authority, wishing to prove and to see all things. Hence the temper of Humanism, man entering into his kingdom and turning his eyes away from faith and the supernatural. Hence a reaction from the *secular* mediæval tradition, each nation and race standing on its own ground and vindicating its independence against the rest of Christendom.[1]

If the Church had been in a conquering mood, as she was a thousand years before, all this new expansion of knowledge and power could have been brought into the service of the Christian spirit, and instead of a break with the mediæval tradition there would have been an harmonious, if swift, development, and Christian civilisation would have attained its majority. But, on the contrary, she was then in a weakened condition after an age of schism and under

---

[1] Note the contrast Dawson is drawing here between the mediæval polities of a culturally united Christendom, and the autonomous identities of the inchoate national states.

the invasion of the secular spirit. It was the old story – two much lump and too little leaven. And so the revolt from the old tradition became a revolt from the Church. mediæval civilisation was the result of the marriage of the culture of the Lower Empire to the Northern barbarians; when Western Europe in her expansion outgrew that culture, the Northern nations threw off not only the mediæval tradition, but also the Christianity that had come to them with it, and as it was not possible that they should relapse immediately to their original paganism they fashioned a new Christianity—a transition religion—founded on private judgment and a new legalism. The Church was no longer an independent organism, but became an aspect of the State, and Christianity was thoroughly socialised and moralised.

In Latin Europe, of course, no such new edition of Christianity was possible, and there the reaction was in the direction of Paganism and Naturalism *sans phrase*. In the 16th century the Christian made a renewed and sustained effort to reconquer the ground that had been lost and to continue the Christian social condition in the altered state of Europe. The Church indeed was reformed and society was re-christianised to a considerable extent. In two of the great national States at least the new order was infused with the Christian spirit, and perhaps the Middle Ages themselves cannot show such *remarkable instances of Christian societies as 17th century Quebec and Paraguay*; but the work never went beyond social life, the Counter-Reformation was unable to conquer either thought or art. It could, it is true, use the art and literature of the time in the service of Catholicism as 17th century Rome shows, but it could not inspire them with its own spirit as it had done in the past. In thought and in science Humanism progressed, though society was still Catholic, and hence the dark and repressive aspects of the Catholicism of that age which are in such contrast to the temper of the mediæval Church.[2] The tremendous strain of dominating society spiritually without intellectual or aesthetic help could not but be exhausting, and it is not altogether fanciful to trace the decline of Spain and Italy at least in part to the effects of this superhuman effort.

After the death of Louis XIV. the counter-Reformation finally collapsed. The destruction of the Society of Jesus made it patent to all. It is in the 18th century that the modern world began. In the first place it is the age of Frederick the Great and Joseph II. The great State becomes all-powerful. It will brook no limits to its authority in religion or in any other matter. It will recognise no end but its own

---

[2] That is, the dark aspects of 17th century European Catholic reality stand in contrast to the relatively open and diverse temper of the mediæval Church.

advantage.[3] Consequently the last remains of the Christian commonwealth of mediæval Europe disappear. The supreme violation of natural justice and right between nations is perpetrated by the partition of Poland. Further, in all Catholic countries the rights of the Church are overthrown. As an age of confiscation it rivals or surpasses the 19th century. Everywhere there is a subordination of the Church to the State, a denial of the rights of the Holy See. Gallicanism and Febronianism[4] are everywhere triumphant.

The eighteenth century witnesses a new outburst of Humanism of a definitely anti-Christian kind. The free thought of the Encyclopædists becomes the dominant intellectual force in Europe. The prevalent ideal is to pull down everything and to re-erect an edifice of a new society based on principles of obvious utility. The weapon of ridicule is used against Faith with tremendous effect.

Also there is a new movement of sentimental naturalism, of which Rousseau is the prophet, which at

---

[3] Compare the spirit of the Counter-Reformation monarchy as shown, *e.g.,* in the political testament of Charles II of Spain, "to govern rather by motives of religion than by consideration of State and Policy, preferring the service of God and the Faith to their own advantage." "In order to preserve, maintain, and defend the Catholic Religion his glorious predecessors have employed and even pledged their royal patrimony, preferring the honour and glory of God and of His holy Law to their temporal interests." He recommends his successor "to be very jealous for the Faith and perfectly obedient to the Holy Apostolic See; to live and act always as a Catholic prince." The Bourbons, both in France and Spain, hold an intermediate position which corresponds to the Gallican party in the Church.

[4] Both movements that sought to diminish the power of the papacy in favour of local (France & Germany, respectively) State civil authority.

least gives naturalism a hold on the affections and rouses enthusiasm. Finally there comes the Revolution which is inspired by these ideas. It sweeps away all the debris of the old order, its traditions good and bad, and builds up a new society founded on democracy and freedom of thought. In the wars of the Revolution France becomes the crusader of this new order, and in the course of the nineteenth century the same movement, united with the spirit of nationality, makes a triumphant reappearance in country after country on the Continent. This movement still survives as Continental Liberalism. It is of course a mistake to think that this movement was primarily a popular one. Its main strength was always in the bourgeoisie. The extraordinary resistance that the *Lazzaroni* of Naples made to the French army in 1799 shows what a strong hold the old order still had on the populace. Even in France Brittany, La Vendée, and large districts in the centre resisted the Revolution, and wherever there was a strong and independent Catholic peasantry the Revolution was met by force of arms.

When the rulers of the *ancien régime* understood the danger of the new ideas, they also rallied to an interested defence of the tradition that they had done their best to destroy in the eighteenth century. But it was not Talleyrand and Metternich, but the Basques and the Tyrolese who were the real enemies of the new spirit. Owing to the way in which modern history is written few people are aware of the obstinate resistance of the mediæval tradition in various parts of Europe and America, a reaction which has had its heroes *(e.g.,* Garcia Moreno, La Rochejacquelin, Andreas Hofer) no less than the Revolutionary movement. Even on the threshold of the twentieth century the political testament of Don Carlos embodied the mediæval tradition in its most uncompromising form, and this still commands the allegiance of a considerable Spanish party. It is possible that the fight between the Revolution and the partially revived mediæval tradition might not have been altogether unequal if the combatants had been left to themselves. In fact, however, the Revolution received an ally more powerful than itself which had been growing to maturity in Protestant Europe.

The development of the new order in England had been continuous from the sixteenth century, and consequently the revolutions that were inevitable to its progress were not cataclysmic as was the great Revolution in France. The new non-feudal land-owning class, which had attained such power at the Reformation, set itself to conquer political supremacy during the seventeenth century. By 1688 it had succeeded in finally vanquishing the old tradition and the claims of authority by divine right in Church and State, and had set up an oligarchic republic under monarchical forms. Thenceforward the energies of the ruling class and the new classes that followed it were devoted not to the destructive work of the contemporary "liberal" movement in France, but in accordance with the national temperament to the practical work of developing the resources of the country in wealth and material prosperity. The freedom that they had vindicated against the Crown was not, as is popularly taught, the freedom of the individual against arbitrary power, for the poor man was better protected under the old order; it was, on the contrary, the *security of the de facto social powers in the nation from interference by a de jure authority.* The dominant interest should not be restricted in its free development by anything but the constraint of a more powerful interest, so that the dominant social forces became ends in themselves and society was freed from the constraint of a distinctive *a priori* policy.

This system had its obvious disadvantages; the poor were at the mercy of the ruling classes, so that the Revolution was the death-knell of the English yeomanry; but in a time of expansion and of new opportunity in industry and trade, it gave a tremendous material advantage to England. English commerce set out to conquer the world, agriculture was placed on a capitalist basis; above all, industry was revolutionised and the age of Iron began. In eighteenth-century England modern capitalism and industrialism were born. Naturally the Whig oligarchy were not able to maintain their rule through all these changes, for as the new interests became strong they also vindicated their claim to free development. First, the American colonies refused to be governed in the interests of the mother country, and with similar traditions to the English started their gigantic development.

Later, the capitalists and industrial magnates claimed a share in the English polity, and after a struggle lasting through a great part of the nineteenth century definitely defeated the agricultural interest.

But as the peasants had been sacrificed to the landlords, so were the artisans to the manufacturers, who claimed the right to exercise their economic strength to the full. Consequently industrial development went on with the same reckless waste of human material that had marked Roman capitalism in the Iron Age of the Republic, and the mill towns and mining villages in England became a byword through Europe for squalor and misery.

Amidst this growing materialism of social life English Protestantism had made gallant efforts to retain or revive some form of Christianity, but as they could make no effort to convert society and to inspire it with their own spirit all their efforts were doomed to failure. Wesley himself in later life confessed the impossibility of keeping his converts from the spirit of the world. The Methodist he describes, whose regularity of life and probity were helps to money making, was a common character in the England of the eighteenth ands seventeenth centuries. Consequently Protestantism tended to more and more to make men conscientious members of the existing society—good citizens—and the supernatural character of religion gradually disappeared.

English Liberalism, which itself owed a great deal to Protestantism, became in the nineteenth century the characteristic mode of thought of industrial England. It was marked by an entire faith in the indefinite progress of material prosperity by industry and trade, and in the complete satisfactoriness of this progress as the aim of human society and the last end of man.

In the nineteenth century, and especially since 1870, all the currents that we have been describing have begun to flow into one another, and to form the majestic river of modern civilisation. To the German Empire belongs the credit of reconciling the Great State with the Industrialism and Capitalism which had been accompanied in England by an almost anarchic individualism, but the German Empire retains something of the old *regime* in its royal and aristocratic hierarchy. The results of the German system are, however, being adopted by all the modern great Stares, even by England and the United States, for the unrestricted individualism of the early nineteenth century could not have continued to develop without bringing with it the break-up of society itself.

In the same way the intellectual and democratic Liberalism of France, the heir of the spirit of Revolution, has been amalgamated, both on the Continent and in England and the United States, with capitalism and the idea of the great State; and the spirit of humanism and faith in the possibilities of science have given to the whole complex a culture and almost a religion of its own.

The amalgamation is, however, by no means complete. There remains an opposition between the capitalistic plutocracy and the revolutionary democracy, and also the opposition between Nationalism and Cosmopolitanism. The Socialism which was produced in Germany in the last century made an effort to overcome these inconsistencies; it based itself uncompromisingly on the secularist spirit and on the idea of the great State as the one all-sufficient end of man – a society all-powerful and all-embracing. But Socialism was weakened by the Utopian character of its aims and hopes; it under-estimated the hold of the plutocracy on that system of representative government which had been the great creation of the nineteenth century revolutions, and in its endeavour to capture the legislative machinery it was itself caught in the wheels and rendered harmless. Nevertheless it has had a most powerful influence on the mind of the age, and though the Socialist party itself may be a Samson grinding the corn of the Philistines, the march of events can hardly fail to fulfil its essential idea, whether by the destruction of the plutocracy and the rise of a real democracy which can organise capital and industry for itself, or, as seems most probable in England at present, by the plutocracy converting itself into a bureaucracy and thus making itself a necessary part of the Great State.[5]

With regard to the other question of the opposition between Nationalism and Cosmopolitanism we seem, as I write, to be assisting at the dying struggles of the Balance of Power, and it is difficult not to believe that sooner or later the world-civilisation of our age will develop an international organisation capable of being its political embodiment.

Whatever development the future may bring, the character of our civilisation is clear enough even in the present. We are face to face with a society, substantially the same in every State, compared to which

---

[5] *Editor's note:* we can see now over 100 on after the original printing of this article, how true this turned out to be.

the Roman Empire was a bagatelle. In its centralisation, its wealth, its hold over its members, its economic and financial organisation, it is unlike anything the world has ever seen. No wonder that the man who looks only at the exterior believes that our age is incomparable and that its wisdom is the only wisdom for man. No wonder that the will and spirit of this society have become a god whom no man dares to question. What society can dare to defy this world and hope to live? Yet we must believe that the Church will conquer, if we cannot believe that the spirit of this civilisation is the Spirit of Christ and of His Church. It is true that this society does not possess a false religion or false views of the supernatural, as did the ancient world. But it has a negative and even hostile attitude to the supernatural. It will accept and honour a religion which consists in enjoining social duty on men, but it will have nothing of a theory of life which subordinates this world and its prosperity to the next. The present order is an end in itself; what helps the present order is good, what hinders it is bad. That is the substance of the social creed. Consequently worship of success and of money, which at last acquires an almost sacramental importance. Nor is this by any means confined to gross and common minds.

It is a creed that can be idealised, and moreover the world will gladly use real virtue and self-sacrifice so long as its great ends are not impeded.

If we are inclined to pessimism the outlook must seem dark indeed. for it would seem that if Catholics remain faithful to the spirit of the Church, they will dwindle to a small and persecuted minority. If they retain numbers and worldly power, they will become weakened and subdued by the dominant spirit of society. But we know that God is never nearer His Church than when she seems to men to be most forsaken, and therefore we can go forward in faith, doing what is humanly possible and leaving the rest to the Holy Spirit. Nevertheless, unless a miraculous conversion of the spirit of the age takes place, we must expect the Church for a considerable period to occupy somewhat the same position as it did in the Pagan Roman Empire; we must resign ourselves to the prospect of a new age of the catacombs, a period of hidden and perhaps persecuted activity, in which the Church will work once more to convert the world and which we may hope will end, as in the ancient world, with her victory and triumph. Whatever the outward results may be, we cannot doubt that the divine leaven will work. However strong a society may be, the needs of the individual soul exist, and all Nature, much less a great material civilisation, is incapable of satisfying them. We cannot hope that the successful, the powerful, and the wise will turn to the Church, for they are just those who find satisfaction for their souls in the kingdom of this world ; but, as from the first, the Kingdom of God will be preached to the poor and the unsatisfied, those for whom the world has no use and those that it uses callously as its slaves. And the more complete is the material triumph of this civilisation the less there will be to hope for, and the greater void will there be in men's souls.

Christopher Dawson, 1915

2

THE PASSING OF INDUSTRIALISM[6]

THE war[7] presumably marks the end of an age no less decisively than did the wars of the French Revolution. In this case, however, it is not a venerable and moribund society like the *Ancien Regime* that is passing away, but a transitional order, which was essentially a compromise and which never attained to a mature and consistent development.

Will the new age be a continuation of the main tendencies of the 19th century or a reaction against them? Will the world continue to "progress" in the old Liberal sense, or shall we witness a return to older principles which have been falling into discredit for the last few centuries? Those who incline to the latter view are already numerous in England; but the popular belief in the infallibility of "progressive" principles is still hardly touched.

The last age was essentially a time of violent and destructive change. It doubtless resembled, on a far

---

[6] In this essay, Dawson identifies the beginning of the end of the modern industrial age, and proposing a new kind of social organisation that can replace that of the Leviathan industrial state, namely, what we might call the *Co-operative Principle* of social organisation.

[7] *i.e.* World War I

larger scale, the hundred years of disorganisation and expansion in the Ancient World which preceded the establishment of the Roman Empire. And like that period it was necessarily transitory. It can only be explained as the transition state between one relatively stable order of society and another; in the one case from the city-state to the Roman Empire, in the other from mediæval society to what we may hope is a new world order.

The last age was an age of exploitation and therefore its duration was limited; it was not simply a case of the exploitation of the weak by the strong as in the last age of the Roman Republic; it. was the exploitation of the world and of its resources *by man*. The natural riches lying unused for ages were spent recklessly for the sake of immediate advantage *without thought of the future*. It was the case of a pigmy, with the mind and aims of a pigmy, suddenly endowed with the power of a giant. In England the whole powers of the nation were thrown recklessly into the struggle for exploitation. The welfare of the people, the moral law, were thrown aside in order that the newly discovered riches could be made profitable; that the iron and coal and cotton could be put on the world market, and the riches of the exploiters increased. Thus there was not only no spiritual purpose in the process – there was not even a worthy human end. On the immense suffering and labour of the people was built up the hideous edifice of Victorian industrial society.

The men of that age did not realise that this process could not last. They accepted the industrialisation of England and the wealth that sprang from it as a natural consequence of the freedom of society and trade. England was in the nature of things fitted to be the workshop of the world, though other nations might follow her progress at a distance, and there could be no question but that the new order was desirable and permanent. In reality the note of the time was not freedom, but conquest and exploitation. England had gained an advantage over the rest of the world by the evolution of the new industry and capitalism and of the new *entrepreneur* class, while the rest of Europe was absorbed in war and politics, and also by her naval and colonial supremacy, and for many years the whole world was economically at her mercy. Lancashire and Birmingham obtained an artificial and temporary command of the markets of the East, and the new world became a great plantation from which the British factories drew their raw material.

The industrialisation of England was completed in the latter part of the 19th century when her dependence on the home food supply was eliminated by the development of steam transport. Henceforward she was truly cosmopolitan, existing for and supported by the world market, and agriculture ceased to be of national importance either socially or economically. But by the time this had happened England was no longer the one great workshop of the world. The nations of the continent and the U.S.A. had revolted against the economic supremacy of England, and had organised themselves afresh so as to gain a share in the new industry and in the world trade that had made her rich. The industrialisation of the continent, however, was built up not on the optimistic free-trade individualism which had established itself in Great Britain half a century earlier. Protective tariffs, organised educations, and labour legislation were all co-ordinated by the State to one end. The economic powers of the nation were concentrated so as to give one another mutual support; and the race between the nations for industrial efficiency and commercial supremacy, went hand in hand with the increase in armaments and the struggle for military power. The world was too small for the gigantic development of the new industrial powers, and in every market they jostled and undercut one another for an opening. No country was too small or too backward to join in the race, and even the Oriental nations began to take their part. The old distinction between manufacturing and agricultural lands tended to disappear, and even in the new countries of N. America and Australasia industrialisation outstripped agrarian development. Almost every nation became obsessed by the idea of using the resources of its own territory solely for its own enrichment. So that while industrialism is becoming ever more universal, the international markets are becoming relatively more restricted.

The economic supremacy, first of 19th century England, then of Western Europe, was based on a monopoly of industrial skill and capital and on an unlimited supply of cheap raw material. Prairie farming — i.e., the cheap and wasteful cultivation of great spaces of fertile virgin soil — rendered possible the cheap food supply, which in turn permitted low wages and cheap labour. But already this state of things is coming to an end. So rapid has been the process of development, so quickly has the increase of population answered the stimulus of the new conditions that extensive agriculture even before the war was becoming out of date. Even in the prairies of the Western states land was becoming sufficiently valuable to repay careful cultivation, and the price of corn and meat was rising steadily.

The vacant spaces of the earth are not yet filled, but they are already limited and the end of the process is in sight. The new world of five continents is becoming a closed and settled area like the old world of Southern Europe and S. Asia; and once again there begins the severe pressure of great nations on territory and food supply. The limitation of the future is not one of industrial skill and capital, but one of raw materials. As population advances, the price of raw materials must increase, while, owing to the growing perfection of organisation and machinery, there is practically no limit to the reduction in costs of manufacture. In the long run the valuable capital will not be machinery or the labour which can work it, for these can be found everywhere, thanks to the spread of industrialism, but the produce of the soil, the amount of which is essentially limited. Thus there will be a tendency for agriculture to recover the place that it lost in the 19th century and to become once more the basis of national prosperity. The need for intensive cultivation will involve the concentration of more money, more labour and more thought on agriculture. The peasant, who was in 19th century England an unimportant and neglected member of society, will doubtless become influential, and will demand a larger share in the produce of his labour. No land will be poor enough to be neglected, or rich enough to be cultivated wastefully. The aim of the agriculture of the future will be the maximum produce rather than the maximum net profit, and every productive possibility will have to be developed to the full. This will involve the increase of the agricultural population in all the regions of the New and Old World where intensive cultivation is not already the rule, and points ultimately to the growth of a new territorial self-sufficiency. This process is already at work in the U.S.A. and there is a tendency in some districts for the old large-scale pioneer wheat farming to yield place to the small holdings and intensive culture of the Italians and Portuguese.

At the same time the causes which led to the formation of great centres of industrial population have begun to diminish. The growing importance of water power favours a new type of industrial settlement, and the transmission of power by electricity makes it no longer necessary for the great factory towns to be huddled together at the mouths of the coal pits.

It is obvious that these two factors which make for an equal distribution of population cannot easily or quickly take effect on so highly industrialised a country as England. They act first on the new countries where conditions are more plastic. Nevertheless it is difficult to exaggerate the importance of the economic world-change that they foreshadow.

The third factor which is making for a new social order, is the human one, and nowhere is it more insistent than in England. The disaffection of the wage labourer on whom the industrialist system rests, endangers the solidity of the whole edifice; and *this* disaffection is not simply discontent with hard conditions or low wages, it is an intellectual and spiritual dissatisfaction with the present social system, and a demand for a new life. This spirit is a necessary product of the transitional state of society which characterised the 19th century. Industrialism involved the destruction of the hierarchic economic and social order of the old regime, and it was therefore forced to ally itself with the political liberal movement which preached the rights of the individual and the abolition of privilege. It was inevitable that the worker, who had been fed on democratic political theories, should come in time to demand a corresponding adjustment of economic and social conditions. He demanded full citizenship.

Hitherto every form of society has limited the true citizen class to a minority. Civilisation has been built up on the foundation of a slave or helot class which did not exist for itself but was the instrument of the dominant race or class.

In the middle ages, it is true, the real slave class disappeared, and even the peasant came to have a half citizenship. The craftsmen of many of the free towns and the peasants of certain exceptional regions attained integral political and economic freedom. Taking West Europe as a whole, however, the true citizen under the old regime was the noble (*generosus*).

The period of revolution produced the anomaly of political advance and economic retrogression. The new industrial society was constituted once more on a basis in effect, servile. The function of the wage labourer, like that of the slave, was instrumental. He possessed control neither over his work nor its fruit, but remained a human tool in the hands of the *entrepreneur* and the middleman. This state of things was felt instinctively by the worker and held consciously by the reformer to be unnatural in that it meant the subordination of the higher to the lower.

If we look on the present labour movement simply from the point of view of Class War, the prospect is hopeless enough. The victory of capitalism and the reign of blind repression, or the triumph of anarchy and confiscation, or the alternate dominance of either tendency, would each be equally possible and equally disastrous.

But the modern revolt of the worker is not simply a case of the struggle between the "Haves" and the "Have Nots," the Rich and the Poor; it is rather an attempt to reverse the subordination of the human to the mechanical and the creative to the commercial function; and however stormy may be the period of change, we may be sure that a permanent social order can only be attained by the recognition of the human end and the reorganisation of the economic process on that basis.

The ideal of the new order will (let us assume) be the substitution of co-operation for competition. Avoiding the sacrifice and exploitation of men, or the waste of natural resources, in the race for wealth, the economic organisation will be directed towards the all-round development of the resources of the society. The tendency of the industrial age was to consider reward rather than work, to judge everything in terms of money. Men worked in order to get rich, and the state of being rich was an absolute end which need not serve any other social purpose – a kind of Nirvana. In this, as in other things, that age subordinated the human to the material.

On the other hand in the Middle Ages, and in many other periods of a more stable social order, social status was inseparable from function. The knight's land and the merchant's money existed like the endowments of the abbeys and colleges, in order to enable them to fulfil their office. A man who had great wealth and no function was an anomaly, and so also to a lesser degree was the man who had a function and no means with which to fulfil it.

Will not the new age be marked by a return to these principles? A man's position will be determined by his function rather than by his possessions, and wealth will be subordinate and instrumental to work. Thus capital will be regarded not as an abstract entity but as so much apparatus, and unless State socialism should succeed in nationalising the means of production, the apparatus would normally be owned by the men who use it, while the higher non-economic functions would be provided for, as in the Middle Ages, by endowment.

Postulating the incipience of this social and economic reorganisation the problem one foresees is this – will it proceed directly from the State, or from the free association of individuals? i.e., will the ideal of

State socialism or that of voluntary co-operation prevail?

The former ideal was essentially a product of the industrial age. It was based on a belief in the superiority of the industrial centralisation of the large scale business, and presupposed an industrial type of society in which agriculture was of little relative importance. It was an answer to the question, How can the lives of the workers be made tolerable if the economic conditions of the 19th century industrial State are to continue? And it made no attempt to restore true economic freedom and self-determination to the individual. The exaggerations of the *laissez faire* school had caused a profound distrust of all individualism, popular faith in Parliamentarism was still unexploded, and there was as yet no realisation of the dangers of a pseudo-democratic Servile State.

The last generation, however, has seen the growth of bureaucracy and the extension of government control in all departments of life, and an increasing distrust of politics and politicians among the people, and there is a general recognition of the necessity for a different type of guidance and direction if democracy and freedom are to be anything but a sham. Moreover, though the centralised socialist State may make for efficiency, it could hardly make for harmonious world development, unless the dream of a single world State were realised. The existence of a number of socialist centralised States each perfectly organised internally, and independent with regard to one another, would on the premises lead to the continuance of the present state of national rivalries and war.

Is not the co-operative ideal that which best meets the needs of the new order ? The substitution of all-round world development for the exploitation of the world by the industrial powers, the gradual equalisation of conditions between the old world and the new, and between the industrial and agricultural countries, as well as the dominance of the new humanist-democratic ideal, all make in the direction of decentralisation and free association rather than of the unitary State and bureaucratic control.

The co-operative theory conceives the State, not as a mechanico-political unit under the control of the sovereign, whether autocratic or democratic, but as a living organism in which each part has its own function and develops according to its own laws.

Thus citizenship is a manifold thing. The individual is not simply a member of the State; he belongs to other corporate unions according to the function which he performs and the locality in which he dwells; and as the guild or union of which he is a free partner is bound to respect his rights, so surely is the State bound to respect the rights of the corporate entities of which it consists.

Functional unions, *i.e.* the associations of members of a particular trade or profession, are not the only corporate bodies which make up the State. The territorial and inter-functional units are of even greater importance, since they possess the capacity for a political and social life of their own.

During the past age the centralised State and centralised industry tended to absorb all local life into the great urban conglomerations, and brought about a separation between the town and the country which paralysed rural life and gave an unhealthy and one-sided development to the city. On the other hand, the general economic tendencies of the new age which we have discussed, all point towards a revival of local life. The more equal distribution of population and industrial development together with the revived importance of agriculture will restore the connection between the city and the agricultural districts which surround it, and the city will tend to become again what it was before the industrial revolution – the centre and head of a natural region rather than the offshoot of a cosmopolitan organisation which has little in common with the country life which environs it.

The co-operation and mutual interpenetration of town and country would benefit both the countryman and the town worker, and would help to produce a new local patriotism and civic life.

There is, to be sure, a certain competition between the federation of unions for the same function in different regions, and the federation of the different functional unions in one region and city. But adjustment has to be sought in the principle that the local citizenship should come before membership of the general functional union, and that the primary functional unions should consider themselves as members of the regional society even more than of the national or international federation of the unions of their own trade. Thus the co-operative State, like the Roman

Empire, would be a federation of local organisms, each possessing a civic life of its own, but it would begin where the Roman Empire left off, with a common citizenship and equal rights of development for all its members. Moreover from the co-operative point of view the national State is not, as the last age believed, the one absolute society, its position and powers are interdependent and related to the other corporate unions. As there are societies with rights below it so there are societies with rights above it, though these ate as yet unrealised. As the national culture existed to a great extent before the national state, so the international culture exists before the international state.

In modern times the claims of international society have been represented by a somewhat thin and narrow cosmopolitanism. The strength of the Nationalist movement of the 19th century was due to its being based on a sense of the past and on a deep and rich conception of the national tradition, while the typical internationalist too often tended to despise the spiritual heritage of the past and concentrated his attention too much on the mechanical adjustments of the industrial and scientific movement, and in general on the material progress which was transforming the world. Their conception of the new age was, so to speak, apocalyptic. They looked for the coming of a new culture which would be absolutely a new departure – a break in spiritual tradition. As there was an unbridgeable gulf between the steam engine and the horse, so it seemed to them there could be nothing in common between the old civilisations based on religious ideals and the new material rationalist culture. The Englishman and the Hindu, putting off the old man and his superstitions, were to enter, newborn, on equal terms, into the Kingdom prepared for them by Adam Smith and Herbert Spencer.

This habit of mind, if it still survives, is not characteristic of the present age.[8] The most sceptical and the least traditionalist begin to realise that the new mechanism of our civilisation has to make adjustment with the more perennial spiritual forces which have created every culture since the world began. That the great spiritual traditions of the past, in religion, philosophy and art are not only still alive, but stand out as the dominant realities of life, is becoming increasingly realised. And with that perception comes the problem of developing and applying these living realities with the greater powers and further knowledge we now have.

Any attempt to substitute an artificial cosmopolitan civilisation for the cultural traditions which have moulded the thoughts and the lives of peoples for ages, not only makes for spiritual impoverishment and superficiality, but even reacts on the physical existence of a people.

European civilisation of the 19th century type has proved a more deadly enemy to the native races which have been fully exposed to its influence, than famine, disease or war, and it has had a profoundly depressing

---

[8] *Editor's note:* We might smirk a bit at young Dawson's naïveté here, but his point of view aligns with other great thinkers such as Berdyaev and Guardini, even if he is a bit soon in his estimation of when such a societal shift will take place – and how long it will take to come into being.

effect even on races of high civilisation, such as the Burmese or the Egyptians.

On this account it is seen that missionary activity must work from within by grafting a new spirit on to the traditional culture. Any attempt to convert people of a different race by dressing them in trousers and teaching them the phraseology of British Liberalism is to create a being false to its own instincts, which must be either a monstrosity or a hypocrite. It is true that whole peoples have received a new religion imposed upon them from without, but this it would seem is only possible in the case of a really theocratic society, like Islam.

The true internationalism, like the true nationalism, bases itself on real social entities, which have been evolved in the course of ages. Everywhere we find local and national societies bound together by spiritual and cultural conditions which form them into a single civilisation. Such civilisations are real societies which demand real loyalty from their members; and the relations of the nations towards them are similar to those of the counties and provinces to the national States of the Middle Ages. Underlying them there is usually a religion as in the case of the great church-State, Islam, which is the most typical of all, but sometimes their basis is predominantly secular, as in the case of China.

These civilisations are the ultimate social realities and in the past they were like closed worlds which were hardly conscious of each other's existence. In the present age, however, the most complex of all these civilisations – that which was developed in the

Mediterranean world and Western Europe has attained to a world hegemony, and the other world cultures are more or less submitted to its influence.

It thus occupies a somewhat similar position to that which Hellenism attained among the cultures of the ancient world, and it may become in the future, as Hellenism did, the parent of a world civilisation. Its first duty, however, lies towards itself. The international anarchy, which has been growing worse since the Renaissance and during the very centuries in which the organisation of the national societies has been perfected, needs bringing to an end, and the society of nations of European civilisation, in the old world and the new, calls for the fullest recognition.

This, however, is not a simple problem. It is true that our civilisation is the direct descendant of both the Roman Empire and mediæval Christendom, and consequently has a religious as well as a political unity behind it, but this unity has been rent in pieces by racial and religious schism. The great divisions of Europe: the Latin, the Germanic and the Slavonic or East Slav peoples, each possess a different spiritual tradition, and are only united by the secular culture of modern Europe. The great question of the immediate future is how far the international spirit can overcome these greater divisions as well as national and local particularism.

The heaviest responsibility to the new age lies, it would seem, upon Great Britain. The peculiar intermediate position historically and geographically which she occupies between the Latin and the Germanic peoples and between the Old World and the

New, allocates to her a high rôle in the building up of an international order. As we have seen, the future of the world rests very largely on the great agricultural territories of North and South America and Australasia. And of these the greater parts are being filled up rapidly by English-speaking people, moulded by British institutions.[9] If England were to conceive her mission in a narrow nationalistic sense, and were to attempt to organise her empire as a self-sufficient whole over against other national empires, the result could in the end hardly be other than disastrous. She is a trustee for Europe – at least for that part of Europe which cannot reproduce its culture in South America or Siberia, and it is her duty to prepare the new lands to receive the full European heritage through the contribution of the different national cultures.

This does not, of course, imply the creation of a cosmopolitan population in the colonies. The indiscriminate mixture of different races and nationalities brings with it the loss of social personality and only the worst elements are apt to survive. While English, Irish, and Scandinavians can unite fruitfully in a new environment, the immigration of peoples of widely different race or civilisation, *e.g.* the Polish Jews or the Armenians, causes acute social indigestion.[10] The

---

[9] Dawson did not foresee here the shift in power from the UK to the USA that was already underway and reached completion during the Second World War, just as in a similar way today, many people do not see the shift in global power away from the USA and on to one or another rising global power.

[10] What Dawson means by this phrase is simply that widely different cultures have a difficult time genuinely integrating together.

United States, which are, *par excellence,* the creation of the Exploitation period, are a remarkable example of the dangers of this state of things, and the problem of the assimilation of the Slav, the Levantine and the Jew is hardly less acute than that of the Negro in the Southern States.[11]

Instead of immigrants from every corner of Europe being poured pell-mell into the great cities and industrial districts of the new-world, each region should he settled deliberately, on the basis of its natural possibilities and the character of its actual population.

These are among the great problems that lie before the new age; but one fundamental question remains to be discussed on which the whole possibility of the co-operative ideal depends.[12] If guidance, direction, control are to be distributed so that each part and organ of society performs its function freely as a living thing, and not part of a machine, there must be a living union, of mind and will between the society

---

[11] Dawson's terminology, and even his concepts here may seem distasteful or even offensive to modern readers, but it is important to note that these were considered pressing concerns by the intelligentsia of the English-speaking world. His example of the African-American in the southern states of the USA is not wrong – the promise of integration and equality that enamoured so many never actually came to fruition, but has only perpetuated (though a number of complex factors) a segregated society marked by intense, if often invisible, racism.

[12] Again, Dawson's Co-operative Principle is not predicated on ethnic or racial categories and assumptions such as he mentions above, but rather these illustrate one application (if in rather poor-taste) of the principle to what in his day were considered legitimate social categories and cultural concerns. At the base of it, Dawson is arguing for harmonious integration of groups and classes across boundaries and levels in a new organic organisation of human society.

and its members, such as we can hardly conceive at present.

Under the old regime society was based on religion, and the unquestioning acceptance by all of one spiritual tradition and one moral ideal was a stronger uniting force than any political authority or organisation.

In the modern State the mind of the average citizen is moulded by the government school and the popular press, and these give him views of life which at best may be called circuitous, and they stir him with ambitions rather than inspire him with ideals.

Religion still claims the right to direct men's lives, but it is to a great extent precluded from direct action on the secular world and is no longer a dominant social force. The ordinary life of the farm and the factory has little contact either with church or school, and so the daily work of mankind has been materialised and rendered both selfish and servile. Education in any real sense should be the nervous system of society, by which the whole organism is guided and kept in union with the spirit. It should be in touch on the one hand with the actual daily life of every citizen, on the other with the higher spiritual ideals which are the end and justification of every civilisation.

Many movements in this direction have already been begun by schools of social reform, which collectively may be called the new humanism, but a profound revolution will have to take place if the present system is to be genuinely transformed.

The idea of a standardised State education, centring round the examinations system, has entered deeply into men's minds, and the blasphemous conception of two educations—the liberal or ornamental, and the mechanical or utilitarian—is still largely dominant in England.

In a truly co-operative State, the school would be vitally and systematically connected first with the social unit that it serves, whether that be an agricultural village or an industrial guild; and secondly, with the larger regional unit or city with its richer many-sided social life, itself equipped with the completer educational institution we call the university. If the one aim of education were the complete and harmonious culture of the whole man, then the intellectual faculty would not as at present be favoured at the expense of either physical, artistic or moral development. And for the full enrichment of personality and community together is needed above all, an education based on a spiritual tradition. Under the present system religious instruction seems to the average man a singularly dead thing, and the question of religious education has come to be treated as a dry bone of sectarian controversy. But the fundamental problem is a very vital one. The spiritual faith and ideals of a man or a society—their ultimate attitude towards life—colour all their thought and action and make them what they are. It is true that the multiple sects of the English speaking peoples are largely historical relics, and no longer represent a fundamental religious attitude. Nevertheless different spiritual traditions do exist, and it is unjust to deprive them of free expression in education and social life. The adherent of the secular tradition which is now perhaps the dominant spiritual force in our civilisation, naturally claims that education should harmonise with *his* view of life, and *his* interpretation of man's history, but only a bigot can demand that the mind of a Catholic or a Quaker should be forced into the same mould. In the long run, the idea of uniform State education is inseparable from a State religion and the penalisation of religious dissent.

A free co-operative order which gives full liberty for the development of man in both his individual and his corporate life must likewise give free play to the spiritual forces by which alone humanity can realise its highest possibilities. The great hope for the future lies, after all, not so much in changes of social organisation as in a spiritual renascence. The curbing of the brutal economic struggle of the industrial age finds its justification not in the equal diffusion of material prosperity which was the goal of the philosophers of the industrial age, but in the opportunity it gives for every member of society to take an active share in the life of the mind and the spirit.

Christopher Dawson, 1920

3

THE EVOLUTION OF
THE MODERN CITY

The problem of the industrial city is so essentially a modem one that we are only just beginning to appreciate its full meaning. In all the centuries since first men began to build cities the world has seen nothing resembling the movement which, in a few generations, has covered whole regions of Europe and America with a black network of towns. At the beginning of the last century[13] the cities of Germany, for example, had hardly changed since the end of the Middle Ages. They were still self-sufficing, separated each by its own customs barrier from the surrounding country; their craftsmen were still bound by the old guild regulations; their citizens were an hereditary caste sharply divided from the nobles on the one hand and the peasants on the other. Of all the 1,000 corporate towns of Prussia only seventeen numbered more than 10,000 inhabitants, while many of them were mere villages of a few hundred souls. By the end of the century the whole face of society was changed. Great industrial cities, number-

---

[13] Writing in 1923, Dawson is here referring to the beginning of the 19th century.

ing their inhabitants by the hundred thousand, were springing up in every part of Germany. The descendant of the eighteenth century serf had become a socialist factory hand or a commercial traveller. Great trusts and cartel's controlling vast resources had taken the place of the old guild regulated handicrafts.

Thus the new industrial movement was nothing less than a transformation of civilisation. The old city life of Europe, which had possessed an unbroken tradition from the age of the Carolingians down to the eighteenth century, had come to an end. The city that was destined to take its place was a new creation without a civic past or any organic connection with the old civic tradition of Europe.

This new type of city first arose in eighteenth century England – that is to say, in the age and the country in which the old city life had become most decadent. In England and in the north-west of Europe generally the city had never become the normal type of social organisation as in the Mediterranean lands. In the latter, civilisation has always preserved the city character imprinted on it by the Graeco-Roman city state. There, even now, the provincial capitals keep much of their vitality as regional centres, and a man's first patriotism still goes to his city. There, too, the educated and ruling classes are almost exclusively city dwelling—the noble no less than the true "bourgeois" —and even the landowner makes his home in his city "palace" rather than his country villa. But in Northern Europe this was never the case. There, the normal social unit has been the village with its centre in the church and the manor house. In the Middle Ages the ruling classes lived isolated in their own fiefs, given up to hunting and war, and despising[14] the inhabitants of the cities as an inferior caste of tradesmen and artisans. And whilst in France and the countries under French influence the Renaissance monarchy gradually changed all this, and converted the nobility into a new class of courtier-townsman, in England the Renaissance monarchy was defeated, and the landed aristocracy gained control of the whole political order. The country squires, the lineal descendants of the mediaeval landowners, still lived on their own estates, with a true feudal contempt of the city, and a more than mediaeval passion for the chase. As Justices of the Peace they were the true rulers of the country; and, as members of Parliament, they absorbed the power formerly possessed by the Court on the one hand, and the yeomanry and the corporate towns on the other. The whole evolution of English society from the seventeenth to the eighteenth century was the inverse of that of the continent: it moved from urban monarchy to rural aristocracy. And it was the England that followed these traditions and was governed by this class that was suddenly precipitated into the full current of the Industrial Revolution.

This alone is sufficient to explain the haphazard and inorganic development of the new towns. The living social organs were those of the national state, and were rural and aristocratic in character. The rulers

---

[14] It's is important to point out the shift in meaning of this word over the century since Dawson's writing; the term in his use here means to 'be not bothered about' or 'pay little heed to', rather than 21st century misuse of the term to mean 'hate'.

of the country looked on the development of the new coal mines and factories in somewhat the same way as a Roman senator would have viewed the work of his slave gangs on his provincial estates – as something outside and below civic life. The mediaeval constitutions of the municipalities were no longer functioning. The craft regulations were mere antiquarian survivals. The body of Freemen had practically disappeared; the essential work of the Common Council was being taken over by the Borough Justices of the Peace, and by a number of anomalous bodies—Paving Commissioners, Police Commissioners and the like—created by special Acts of Parliament. Some of the greatest industrial towns were not even corporate cities. Manchester itself was governed by a manorial court—convoked and presided over by the steward of the Lord of the Manor—right down to 1846. At the beginning of the nineteenth century there were still no resident magistrates, and that great city was as dependent on the authority of the neighbouring county justices as any country village.

Moreover, as the ruling classes were not city-dwellers, there was no opportunity for contact and adjustment between the new raw industrial city and the contemporary standards of civilised living. Even the rich manufacturers themselves did not make a permanent home in the towns which produced their wealth. It was their ambition to climb out of their town into the society of the country, which preserved all its social prestige, even in districts where the material advance of the new towns was greatest. In mediaeval Florence the nobles came into the city, as it grew rich, but in nineteenth century Leeds and Manchester the merchants and manufacturers went into the country. There was none of that civic patriotism which caused the mediaeval merchant to spend so large a proportion of his wealth in the service and adornment of the city. And, in the same way, the semi-servile class of wage-labourers, who formed the true population of the new towns, grew up without traditions or ideals, with no share in the national franchise or in the government of their city. Their standards of life were even lower, and their interests more limited, than those of the rural class from which they had sprung. No doubt the mediaeval artisan had no high standard of life, but at least he shared in the living organic life of his city; and the gulf between his existence and that of the collier or cotton spinner of the later eighteenth century is almost that which separates civilisation from barbarism. The whole life of the mediaeval townsmen, whether rich or poor, was in his city and he took part in the life of the outer world only as a member of the civic organism; on the other hand the rich townsman of the industrial age was primarily a citizen of the national state, while the wage-earner could hardly be reckoned as a citizen at all.

Thus it is useless to seek to understand the rise of the industrial city by looking for an internal process of development, such as we can find in the history of the Greek or the mediaeval city. The new towns were not self-conscious and self-determining societies; they were the organs of a national-imperialist movement of economic expansion. And, as the great age of

Roman imperial expansion brought with it the decay of the old municipal life and a terrible degradation of slave labour, so, too, the industrial movement in eighteenth century England brought with it a similar deterioration, alike in the civic life of the town and in the status of the wage-labourer. The same spirit that manifested itself in the ruthless daring and harsh discipline of the eighteenth century navy, caused the sacrifice of the amenities of life in the new cities to the national wealth. At the cost of two or three generations of pitiless toil on the part of the people, and of demoniac energy on the part of the organisers and employers, England established her position as the workshop of the world.

The true character of this movement has been obscured by the false diagnosis of the economists. For a century after Adam Smith, the preachers of Free Trade and *laissez faire* in industry gave a liberal and individualistic interpretation to a process which was essentially due to half a century of disciplined national effort. The economic freedom that English trade and industry had secured for themselves was not the abstract liberty of the eighteenth century philosophers, it was the freedom of the young giant who strips himself of the armour of antiquated restrictions in order to wrestle more freely with his opponents. The real note of the period was not liberty, but economic conquest and exploitation. England possessed an almost complete monopoly in the new industrial methods and her naval and mercantile power enabled her to find an opening for the new products in all the markets of the world—even in those of India and West Africa—while her potential rivals were still hampered by the old economic restrictions or by the pre-occupation of war and revolution. The economists failed to see that this advantage was essentially temporary. They attributed it to necessary working out of economic laws; and, as they believed in the providentially established harmony between individual gain and national welfare, it was natural for them also to suppose that the British industrial monopoly was ideally adapted to the true needs of humanity in general.

Finally, towards the middle of the nineteenth century, the new system achieved its consummation by the revolution of the means of transport and communication and by the consequent realisation in practice of the economists' ideal of the world market. This change, while bringing an enormous accession of force to the industrial movement generally, had a special importance in the development of the industrial city. All the ancient limitations in the size of a city were removed, and the last links that bound the industrial town to its rural environment were broken. The city now lived entirely for and by the world market. It drew its food from one continent, the raw materials for its industries from another, and exported the finished product, perhaps, to a third.

Thus it was no longer in any sense a part or servant of its own region, nor was it organised primarily as a place for its own citizens to live in. It was a cosmopolitan *ergastulum* for the production of wealth. The desire for gain, which was the creative force behind this new city-development, showed itself in every aspect of its life. Thus the interests alike of the producer and the consumer were subordinated to those of the middle-man, the class of financiers, bankers, brokers and merchants, which represented the vital principle of this order in the same way that the knight and the ecclesiastic represented that of the mediaeval state. And the same spirit governed the actual construction of the industrial town: it was built neither for beauty nor for convenience, but for the immediate profit of the ground landlord and the speculative builder. The exploitation ethos, the spirit of Dickens' Gradgrind and Matthew Arnold's Mr. Bottles, was a very real force during the nineteenth century, and in its time it moulded civilisation in England no less effectually than did the militarist ethos in Prussia.

The typical cities of the industrial age—the Lancashire cotton town of a century ago,[15] the Pittsburg or Chicago of the last generation or the new Russian factory towns of 1914—were like the great mining camps which grew up on the Californian and Australian goldfields: not cities, but fortuitous collections of individuals drawn together to exploit the new source of wealth, and one another, and living in chaotic disorder and discomfort without any thought beyond the gain of the moment. And, as the mining camp gave place in time to a comparatively settled and orderly town, so we can see the industrial order gradually passing into something different.

---

[15] *Nota bene: Dawson wrote this in 1923.*

During the second half of the nineteenth century new factors began to appear, which pointed towards the ending of the period of successful economic monopoly. Industrialism was no longer limited to those societies which had first understood how to apply it profitably; it spread over the world with amazing rapidity. The statesmen and economists of the continental countries realised that the doctrines of *laissez faire* and Free Trade only tended to accentuate the economic inferiority of the less developed countries, and they began to use all the resources of statecraft and science in order to organise and protect the industrial powers of their own nations. Thus there arose the new Germanic type of industrialism—so different in its ordered and bureaucratic co-ordination from the haphazard disorder of our own[16] industrial revolution. Yet this advance was dearly purchased by the growing intensification of international competition and the desperate struggle for markets and colonies, which went hand in hand with the development of vast armaments and culminated in the general European War.

The development of rival industrialisms, like that of rival armaments, is a process which contains in itself the causes of its own destruction. It has become increasingly evident that it is possible for industrial production to expand out of all proportion to the growth of the world markets. The prosperity of industrial England of the Victorian age, with its cheap labour and high profits, rested, on the one hand, on

---

[16] *i.e. British*

the cheap produce of the newly opened farm lands of America and, on the other, on the control of the markets of India and the other lands that were not yet industrialised. The universalisation of industrialism imperils both these factors. No country is now either too old or too new to become an industrial power. The cities of the United States are already almost numerous enough to absorb the harvests of the Middle West: India aspires to industrial self sufficiency and Japan to industrial imperialism. And this vast development of world industry and population makes correspondingly heavy demands on the natural resources of the world. A century ago it might well seem that British coal and American timber would last for ever; but the following generations spent the accumulated wealth of ages with such reckless haste that, by the beginning of the twentieth century, it became clear that the wasteful exploitation of coal and timber, and the extensive cultivation of virgin prairie soils, would have to give place to a policy of conservation, to new methods of economy and to a more intensive agriculture.

Moreover, at the same time that the weaker countries were revolting against the economic exploitation of the great industrial powers, the weaker classes were asserting their right to an equal share in the control and profits of industry. If the wage-earner was never a contented partner in the industrial system, it is only recently that education and organisation have given him the power to make his claims felt. The fluidity and docility of labour were essential factors in the old industrial system, and if labour were to achieve the position of an equal partner in industry it would inevitably give rise to a new system. Behind all the ephemeral phenomena of labour disputes and socialist propaganda there lies a really significant change in social mentality—the revolt of the popular mind against the exploitation ethos and the coming of a new humanist ethos which places vital and aesthetic considerations in front of mechanical and financial ones.

This change had also begun to show itself during the last quarter of the nineteenth century in a widespread movement towards better conditions of life in the industrial town. There was a renewal of the municipal spirit, and men once more began to think of the city as a place to live in and not merely as a place out of which to make money. This spirit showed itself in housing and sanitary reform, in the rise of municipal enterprises and institutions, and finally in the town planning movement. Nevertheless the social reformers, like their contemporaries, the Socialists, did not envisage the possibility of any great change in the industrial movement. They all took the giant city for granted, and thought only of how to make it more habitable. Their attitude towards the rural environment of the city was suburban rather than regional—that is to say they looked on it as so much empty space for town-expansion, not as the social complement of the city with which it stands in organic connection.

It is only during the last twenty years that it has become possible to understand the meaning of the new economic and social factors, and to discern the rise of a new type of industrialism, a "neo-technic order," which brings with it the prospect of a new industrial city. We are witnessing on the one hand that universalisation of industrialism that I have just described and, on the other, an agrarian revival which has restored the prosperity of the continental and Irish peasantry and has given them economic strength to resist the exploitation of the middleman. The same process, in a somewhat different form, is taking place in the United States and Canada, where the farmers are organising themselves both economically and politically. Everywhere the agricultural producer is gaining strength against the urban consumer. Already in Central Europe we have seen the country beginning to take its revenge by exploiting the towns; and the time is not far distant when the giant city, which has no regular source of food supply, but is dependent on the surplus of the world markets, will find its position becoming increasingly difficult.

In the long run, the general levelling-out process that these changes involve will favour a smaller type of industrial city and one that is more in contact with its rural neighbourhood. There is no longer sufficient justification for huddling all the factories of a nation round the mouths of the coal pits. The obvious advantage in saving coal freights is largely counterbalanced by the waste and disorder with which this system has been accompanied; and there are great compensatory advantages, even of the economic order, in the opposite policy of a decentralised industry. If industrialism ever attains stable equilibrium it is probable that every town will possess factories but that the pure factory-town will become a thing of the past. The future is not with the giant hive of cosmopolitan industry but rather with the medium sized city of 50,000 to 100,000 inhabitants[17] which possesses a high industrial development but which is also a true centre to the rural districts in which it is placed. For the more closely a town is knit up with its agricultural environment, both socially and economically, the stronger it will be and the richer will be the resources on which it can draw. Hitherto this contact has been notably lacking. Both in Europe and America there is an extraordinary social and intellectual cleavage between the country and the town—even the small town, like Mr. Sinclair Lewis' "Main Street," which is parasitically dependent on the farmer. But it is hardly conceivable that this cleavage can long continue. In England we already see the effects of the new road transport in bringing the villager into close contact with his country town; and everywhere the worker on the land has so far acquired the tastes and mentality of the townsman that the old peasant life and character, which hardly changed from the fifteenth to the nineteenth century, is now completely vanishing. And this process of interpenetration need not stop with the mere urbanisation of the rustic. As it progresses we may hope that the town will receive as well as give; that it will once more recover its contacts with the country around it and with the natural occupations of

---

[17] Note what Dawson calls a "medium-sized city" here hardly qualifies for a town in much of the 21st century American situation (or indeed that of most Western nations), with their multi-millions of inhabitants.

the countryside for lack of which the industrial town has suffered so grievously.

This brings us close to the ideal of the Garden City, but the Garden City movement in its actual development has tended rather towards the substitution of satellite towns for suburbs rather than towards the creation of regional city centres. It may indeed be questioned whether the latter is possible in so highly developed and thickly populated a country as England, and whether our true policy does not lie in the reformation and development of the existing country towns. Up to the present the problems of the market town have been almost completely neglected; but there is no doubt that a small part of the effort and expenditure that have been spent, both on the improvement of the giant industrial city and on the creation of the garden town, might produce remarkable results if it were applied to a market town like Evesham or to a county centre like Salisbury or York. In the case of most of these towns there are none of the heart-breaking masses of material difficulty which meet the town planner in the great industrial city. They are not an amorphous chaos like the latter. They have preserved their organic form, and there is usually sufficient space for secondary replanning and expansion. The obstacles to improvement are rather moral than material – the dead weight of traditional apathy and the absence of a corporate and civic spirit. And these are mainly due to the conditions of the industrial age which have sucked the vitality from the countryside and from the towns that served it. The passing of these conditions, and the rise of a different type of industrialism, would bring about an economic revival of the lesser towns and consequently a renewal of civic life.

It is true that this country[18] has committed itself to the earlier type of industrialism in so wholesale a fashion that the possibilities of further development are not so great as they are either in the new lands across the seas or in the older countries that were left behind by the Industrial Revolution. Nevertheless agrarian England still exists, and our cities cannot long continue to ignore it. The progress of modern science and modern technique is not hostile, but favourable, to a closer contact between the city and its rural environment. There is every reason to believe that the city of the future, no less than those of Antiquity and of the Middle Ages, will be a regional city – the civic expression of the local society. For the greater is man's control and knowledge of nature the more will he be led to make a full civic utilisation of all the potentialities, both for wealth and life, of the natural region with which his life is bound up.

Christopher Dawson, 1923

---

[18] *i.e. Great Britain*

4

PROGRESS AND DECAY IN ANCIENT AND MODERN CIVILISATION

OF all the changes that the 20th Century has brought, none goes deeper than the disappearance of that unquestioning faith in the future and the absolute value of our civilisation which was the dominant note of the 19th century. That age was as full of war and revolution as any century has ever been, but reformers and rebels alike, from the time of the French Revolution to the days of Mazzini and Garibaldi, all had a robust faith in the inevitable victory of the forces of enlightenment and in the coming reign of the great abstractions – Humanity, Liberty, and Progress. They were all of them good Europeans with an immense belief in the European idea. To their contemporaries they may have seemed dangerous and disquieting, but their ideas were of the same fundamental optimism, as those of the bourgeois Liberals.

The reaction from the optimism and security that we are now experiencing is not, as is often thought, simply a product of the Great War. It was preparing during that period of material prosperity and spiritual disillusionment that followed 1870. It was then that the new industrialism and finance became truly international. Men became conscious that they had destroyed the shackles of the old traditional local despotism only to be faced by an infinitely more formidable power, world-wide in extent and strong enough to use any government as its instrument. The last twenty years of the 19th century was an age of imperialism not only on the Continent of Europe, but across the seas. The spirit of the age was shown alike in the scramble for Africa, and in the vast expansion of American Industrialism.

Hence a growing disaffection both among the subject classes and the subject nationalities, and outside the organised socialist and anti-imperialist movements, there was an even deeper human revolt against the harshness and ugliness of a machine-made civilisation. Not only the Ruskins and the William Morrises[19] but even more the Tolstois and the Dostoievskis preached a radical turning away from the victorious material civilisation of the West, and a return to the past or a flight to the desert. Even these who fully accepted the scientific and material progress of the 19th century came to realise the dangers and instability of the new order. They felt the dangers of social parasitism and physical degeneration in the enormous and growing agglomeration of badly-housed humanity, which everywhere accompanied industrialism. They saw everywhere the destruction of the finer

---

[19] John Ruskin and William Morris are famous 19th century English anti-industrialists, artists, craftsmen, and philosophers. Lev Tolstoi (Tolstoy) and Fyodor Dostoievski (Dostoyevsky) are famous Russian writers and philosophers in their own right.

forms of local life and popular arts and crafts before a standardised mechanical culture, and the havoc that was wrought among the primitive peoples through their exploitation by Western capital. A few even realised the destructiveness of an order which was recklessly exhausting the resources of nature for immediate gain, which destroys forests to produce its newspapers and wastes in smoke irreplaceable coal.

But undoubtedly until the European War 19th century optimism and faith in progress was still generally dominant – it was at least the orthodox dogma.

It was the War, and still more the subsequent period of confusion and disillusionment which made the average man realise how fragile a thing our civilisation is, and how insecure are the foundations on which the elaborate edifice of the modern world-order rests. The delicate mechanism of cosmopolitan industrialism needs peace more than any previous order. If modern civilisation has increased enormously in wealth and power, it has also become more vulnerable. Our civilisation is in danger just because of the amazing progress that it has accomplished during the last century and a half. Just because it is more universal, more highly centralised, more mechanically elaborate, it is exposed to perils of which a more rudimentary culture is hardly conscious. Under the old order it was possible for a country like France to engage in almost continuous wars throughout the 17th and 18th century without causing much disturbance in the general life of the community: under modern conditions war between great nations affects every detail of public and private life. The new system owed everything to the forty years of peace—1870-1910—but it did nothing to ensure their continuance. National rivalries grow more intense, and in modern war the nations do not simply fight against one another: they tear to pieces the nerves and arteries of their common life.

We have seen enough of this process already to admit that the men of the 19th century were altogether too naive and optimistic in their conception of progress. They concentrated all their attention on Progress, and neglected the equally important and social factor of Degeneration. All change was progress, and they conceived this not as the growth of a living organism, but as a number of additions to a fixed sum of knowledge and wealth and political liberty. Thus whatever was the fate of particular societies it was always possible to follow the progress of humanity in the converging lines of individual progress – economic, intellectual and political.

This was the creed of Condorcet and many more of the great minds of the 18th century, but in the course of time it was cheapened and vulgarised into a practical apology for the late 19th century industrial civilisation – a world that was growing larger and louder and richer and more self-confident, but which was at the same time decreasing in vitality and losing its hold on its true cultural traditions.

In reality any sound science of social progress must concern itself first and last with the concrete historical and individual cultures and *not with the achievements of civilisation in the abstract.* For a culture is essentially a growth, and it is a whole. It cannot be constructed artificially, nor can it be divided. It is a living body from the simple and instinctive life of the shepherd, the fisherman and the tiller of the soil up to the highest achievements of the artist and the philosopher. The man of genius is not an absolute and unrelated phenomenon in society, a kind of celestial visitant. He is, in an even more intimate sense than the ordinary man, the product of a society and a culture. Science and philosophy are social products just as much as language is, and Aristotle or Euclid could no more have appeared in China, than could Confucius in Greece. A great culture sets its seal on a man, on all that he is, and all that he does, from his speech and gesture to his vision of reality and his ideals of conduct, and the more living it is, the deeper is the imprint, and the more highly developed is the element of *form* in Society. Hence every culture develops its own types of man, and norms of existence and conduct, and we can trace the curve of the growth and decline of cultural life by the vitality of these characteristic types and institutions as well as by the art and literature in which the soul of the culture finds expression.

In certain periods—for instance, the Elizabethan age or the reign of Queen Anne in England—this element of form is strongly marked, and the characteristic types are numerous and full of vitality; in others—for instance the 3rd century A.D. in the Roman Empire—society seems amorphous and formless. The traditional types have become shadowy and unreal, and the types that are most living (such as the barbarian mercenary, or the Oriental diviner) are alien to the traditional spirit of the culture. Moreover there is a close union between the primary creativeness of the culture in life, and its secondary creativeness in literature and art. Falstaff is as true and characteristic a product of the Elizabethan culture as was Drake, and there is a vital link between the style of Addison and the polity of 18th century England. Thus a parallelism may be traced between the rise and decline of the great literary and artistic styles, and that of the life of the society—or the particular phase of its life—which produced them. The Gothic Cathedral rises, comes to its perfect flowering and fades in unison with the rise and fall of the mediaeval communal development. Baroque architecture and sculpture is equally closely connected with the growth and decay of the counter-reformation monarchies.

A style *lives* not by its abstract beauty or suitability but by its communion in the living culture. When the social tradition is broken, when there is a deliberate choice of styles, as in a modern building contract, true style ceases – there is death. That is why a mediæval building has the same relation to modern Gothic,[20] that a live lion has to a wooden one. The same principle holds good in the case of social and political institutions. Just as an artistic or literary fashion can be adopted in an external and artificial way, as was the case with French taste in the 18th century, or with the modern oriental imitations of Western trade goods, so too can a people adopt the political and social forms of a different culture without having vitally

---

[20] That is, a modern Gothic-revival building. The program of Gothic-revival architecture was a highly debated topic in certain circles of the late 19th - early 20th century.

incorporated them. If this process is carried far enough it may involve the end of the living culture, and that is why it is possible for an abstract and superficial progress to be the mark of a vital decline. When the successors of Alexander covered Asia with municipalities, theatres, gymnasia and schools of rhetoric, they did not turn the Asiatics into Greeks, but they did put an end to the native culture traditions, which lingered on only among poor men and country folk. The great network of municipal institutions with which the Hellenistic princes, and afterwards Rome, covered the subject countries were a mechanical and external creation, as compared with the vital and internal impulse that created the Greek City-State. The same thing may be true of representative institutions, universal education, a daily press and all the other insignia of modern civilisation. We have to consider not merely whether an institution is reasonable or good, but first and foremost whether it is alive. There can be no question, for example, but that the modern representative system as it exists in Germany or Austria or Italy, with its elaborate proportional representation and its universal suffrage is, in the abstract, highly superior to the English Parliamentary system of the 18th century, with its rotten boroughs, its absurd anomalies of suffrage, and its corruption. Yet the latter was the living expression of an age and a people of creative political genius; it was one of the great forces that shaped the modern world; while the latter is without a living relation to its society, and is liable to be set aside, as recently in

Italy,[21] in favour of a more primitive system which is more deeply rooted in the political traditions of the people. Only so long as change is the spontaneous expression of the society itself does it involve the progress of civilisation; as soon as the internal vital development of a culture ceases, change means death.

Anyone looking at the Mediterranean world in the age of Pericles might have thought that the future of humanity was assured. Man seemed at last to have come of age and to have entered into his inheritance. Art, Science, and Democracy were all coming to a magnificent flowering in a hundred free cities; and the promise of the future seemed even greater than the achievements of the present. Yet at the very moment when the whole Mediterranean world was ready to embrace the new knowledge and the new ideals of life and art, when the barbarians everywhere were turning to the Hellenic cities as the centre of power and light, all this promise was blighted. Hellenism withered from within. The free cities were torn asunder by mutual hatred and by class wars. They found no place for the greatest minds of the age—perhaps the greatest minds of any age—who were forced to take service with tyrants and kings. So that at last Hellenic science became domesticated at the court of the Macedonian Pharaohs at Alexandria, and the free cities became the spoil of every successful condottiere.

What was the reason of this sudden blighting of Hellenic civilisation? Not, I think, any of the external

---

[21] i.e. Italy's turn to Fascism in the early 20th century.

causes that have been invoked – the Peloponnesian War, the introduction of Malaria, the exhaustion of the soil. These were at most secondary causes. Nor was it, as Professor Gilbert Murray says in his interesting book on Greek religion, due to a "loss of nerve." It goes deeper than that. Hellenic civilisation collapsed not by a failure of nerve but by the failure of life. When Hellenic Science was in full flower, the life of the Hellenic world withered from below, and underneath the surface brilliance of philosophy and literature the sources of the life of the people were drying up.

As the life passed out of Hellenic civilisation, we see the gradual disappearance of those vital characteristic types in which the spirit of the culture had embodied itself, the passing away of the traditional institutions and the fading of the vivid and highly differentiated life of the regional city-state into a formless, cosmopolitan society, with no roots in the past and no contact with a particular region, a society which was common to the great cities everywhere from Mesopotamia to the Bay of Naples. Hence the degradation of the Greek type. The people is no longer represented by the citizen-soldier, who brought down the power of Persia, but by the "Starveling Greek" of Juvenal's satire, the Jack of all trades from rhetoric to rope-dancing. Instead of the Hellene being by nature the master and the barbarian the slave, we get Persius' centurion, "big Vulfenius," who, "with a guffaw, offers a bad halfpenny for a hundred Greeks."

Yet throughout the period of this vital decline, the intellectual achievements of Hellenic civilisation remained, and Greek culture, in an abstract and standardised form, was spreading East and West far more than it had done in the days of its living strength.

If intellectual progress—or at least a high degree of scientific achievement—can co-exist with vital decline, if a civilisation can fall to pieces from within – then the optimistic assumptions of the last two centuries concerning the future of our modern civilisation lose their validity. The fate of the Hellenic world is a warning to us that the higher and the more intellectually advanced civilisations of the West may be inferior in point of survival value to the more rudimentary oriental cultures.

Yet we need not necessarily assume that our civilisation is fatally bound to go the same way as that of ancient Greece. If we accept Herr Spengler's[22] theory of isolated cultures, each with its fixed life-cycle which it cannot survive, this would indeed follow. But his philosophy, powerful as it is in its realisation of the vital unity of the individual culture movement, fails to take account of the enormous importance of cultural interaction in producing development and change. It was to this factor that the late Dr. Rivers, in consequence of his researches into the history of Melanesian society, came to attribute the whole process of social evolution.

> "I was led," he says, "to the view that the current concept of independent evolution, which I had accepted so blindly, was a fiction. The evidence from Melanesia suggests that an isolated people does not invent or advance, but

---

[22] i.e. Oswald Spengler.

that the introduction (by an immigrant people) of new ideas, new instruments and new techniques leads to a definite process of evolution, the products of which may differ greatly from either the indigenous or the immigrant constituents, the result of the interaction thus resembling a chemical compound rather than a physical mixture. The study of Melanesian culture suggests that when this newly set-up process of evolution has reached a certain pitch it comes to an end, and is followed by a period of stagnation which endures until some fresh incoming of external influence starts anew a period of progress." (*Psychology and Politics*, 118.)

Now in the great majority of cases a change of culture is due to the presence of an immigrant people, and the rise of a new civilisation is the result of the coming of a new people into an old culture-field, for instance the coming of the Dorians and Achæans into the Ægean region, of the Aryans into Northern India, and of the Germanic peoples into the Roman Empire. Consequently the process of fusion and change to which Dr. Rivers refers, extends not only to the culture but to the people itself. We must take account (1) of the action of the new geographical environment on the man and the society that have grown up in another region, (2) of the actions and reactions of the culture of the conquered on that of the conquerors, and (3) finally of the gradual physical mixture of the two peoples. All these factors go to produce the new culture which is neither that of the immigrants nor that of the indigenes, nor a mere position of the two, but a new creation.

Of course culture change is not exclusively racial in origin. As Dr. Rivers suggested, any new cultural element may set up a process of evolution in the society into which it is introduced. We have the case of the introduction of Indian Buddhism into China, which was one of the main factors in producing the Chinese culture of the Tang and Sung periods, but even here it is only fair to point out that some writers explain the new element in Chinese culture as due to the region and people of the Yang-tse valley as against those of the Yellow River, where classical Chinese civilisation originated. In cases such as these, of culture drift, or merely intellectual influence, it is not a new culture that is evolved, but it is the old culture that is developed and enriched. A new and original culture invariably requires new human elements in the society. Moreover, even in the most autochthonous and continuous of culture traditions the element of new blood counts for much. Even in Egypt it may prove to be the case that while the enduring culture tradition is always native, the two great culture cycles, which culminated respectively in the age of the Pyramid Builders and in that of the 18th Dynasty, were set up by the intrusion and assimilation of new racial elements, first in the Delta, and in the second case (from 2700 B.C.) in upper Egypt.

The whole cycle of assimilation and change that goes to build up a new culture appears in most cases to occupy a period of about ten centuries, and it is possible that this remarkable similarity in the duration of culture cycles which has struck so many thinkers, both in the present and in the past, may be due to the process of racial fusion and change requiring a fixed number of generations in which to work itself out.

The formation of a new culture is like that of a race or even of a new species. If it is adapted to the region in which it is placed and to the needs of life, it may persist indefinitely as a stable type; if, on the other hand, it fails to secure this adaptation, it will fade away or collapse. In many cases the passing of a civilisation is connected with the alteration or disappearance of an immigrant stock—its complete assimilation by the conquered people and the new environment. We may trace this process clearly in the history of India. The change from the simple Homeric existence of the warriors and herdsmen of the Vedic age to the world of Buddha, and yet more of Kalidasa, was also a change of peoples. We can see the gradual weakening of the northern stock before Malaria and the countless ailments of the tropics; their powerlessness to preserve homogeneity of physical type in spite of the multiple elaboration of caste restrictions. We can see their healthy straightforward Polytheism being gradually overclouded by the teeming mystery of the tropics, until the men from the North lose their zest for life and turn away with the Buddha from the disheartening endless round of birth and death. Finally, the process ends in the victory of the gods of the land, the Northerners are completely assimilated and their culture tradition is fused with that of the indigenes in the great and characteristically Hindu civilisation of the Gupta period, the mature fruit of the whole Aryo-Indian culture cycle.

The same process of racial or ethnical change is observable in the case of Hellenic civilisation. There is the same gradual adaptation of an immigrant society to a new environment, and the growing preponderance of Mediterranean influence, alike in culture and in blood. But this process is not sufficient by itself to account for the sudden and almost catastrophic enfeeblement of Hellenism in the fourth century B.C. Its premature decline would seem to be due to something analogous to disease in the individual organism. For there is a vital difference between the fixation or stagnation of a civilisation like that of China or Egypt, after the close of its formative and progressive culture cycle, and the organic dissolution of a culture, such as we see in the case of ancient Greece and Asia Minor. The cultures of China and Egypt survived for thousands of years because they preserved their foundations intact. By their fixed and hieratic ordering of social relations they gave to the simplest and humblest functions all the consecration of religion and tradition. But other civilisations have neglected the roots of their life in a premature concentration on power or wealth, so that their temporary conquest of the world is paid for by the degeneration and perhaps the destruction of their own social organs. The most striking instance of this morbid and catastrophic decline—and that which most closely resembles our own condition—is that of ancient Rome in the first and second centuries B.C. Here there was no question of senescence. Society came near to dissolution while at the very height of its cultural activity, when its human types were more vigorous than ever before. The danger to civilisation came not from the decline of vitality, but from a sudden change of conditions – a material revolution, which broke down the organic constitution of the society.

ROME, more than any other city-state of antiquity, was essentially an agrarian state. The foundation of her power and of her very existence was the peasant-soldier-citizen. The lands of the Latin farmers grouped in strategic positions all over Italy, and those of the Roman citizens concentrated in the best land of central Italy, gave the Roman power a broader basis than any other ancient state possessed and differentiated profoundly the Roman legion from the mercenary armies of the Hellenistic states. The peasant religion, the peasant economy and the peasant morale underlie all the characteristic achievements of the republican epoch. But with the conquest of the Mediterranean all this was changed. The peasant-soldier could not be used to garrison Spain or Asia, and his place was taken by a new type of soldier, not as yet mercenary, but at any rate professional. Vast masses of land and slaves were thrown on the market. A new type of agriculture based on the plantation system as it had been worked out in Carthage and the East, gradually took the place of the small yeoman holding. The tribute of Sicily and Asia caused an influx of cheap wheat into Italy which drove home-grown corn out of the market. Finally, there were even greater opportunities for Roman citizens to make great fortunes by speculation, by the exploitation of the conquered peoples and by engaging in the slave and corn trades.

Hence there arose a progressive degeneration and transformation of the characteristic Roman types.

The fundamental peasant-soldier-citizen gave place —as farmer [gave place] to the slave—as soldier [gave place] to the professional—as citizen to a vast urban proletariat living on Government doles and the bribes of politicians. So, too, the noble began to give place to the millionaire, and the magistrate to the military adventurer. Rome became more and more a predatory state that lived by war and plunder, and exhausted her own strength with that of her victims.

Faced by this situation, political circles in Rome were divided between two opposing policies. The conservatives—the men like the Elder Cato—hoped to carry the state through by keeping alive the old Roman tradition and adhering in everything to social and political precedent. The reformers, inspired by the tradition of Greek Radical Democracy, aimed at restoring the citizen class by a drastic redistribution of property among the landless proletariat. Both policies were tried and both ended in disaster. The republic slowly foundered amidst massacres and counter massacres, slave wars and a continual growth of political and financial corruption. It was only by the genius and the persistence of Augustus that Rome regained some hold on her traditions. And even Augustus failed to cure the fundamental malady of the Roman state, though he well realised its importance. He could not restore the citizen farmer in the place of the slave, nor could he cope with the cosmopolitan urban development of the city of Rome itself. For it was literally Rome that killed Rome. The great cosmopolitan city of gold and marble, the successor of Alexandria and Antioch, had nothing in common with the old capital of the rural Latin state. It served no social function, it was an end in itself, and its population drawn from every nation under heaven existed mainly to draw their government doles, and to attend the free spectacles with which the Government provided them. It was a vast useless burden on the back of the empire which broke at last under the increasing strain.

This is an extreme example of the perils that result from the urbanisation of a society, but a similar morbid process can be traced in many other cases of cultural decline.

First comes the concentration of culture in the city with a great resultant heightening of cultural activity. But this is followed by the lowering of the level of culture in the country and the widening of the gulf between townsman and peasant. In some cases, as in ancient Greece, this amounts to a gradual but thorough rebarbarisation of the country, in others—as in Russia since Peter the Great, and in the Hellenistic East since Alexander—the peasants still cling to the traditions of a native culture, while the towns adopt a ready-made urban civilisation from abroad.

In the last stage the cities lose all economic and vital contact with the region in which they are placed. They have become parasitic; less dependant on nature and more dependant on the maintenance of an artificial political and economic system.

It is this process of urban degeneration and not Industrialism or Capitalism or Racial Deterioration or Militarism that is at the root of the weakness of modern European Culture. Our civilisation is becoming formless and moribund because it has lost its roots and no longer possesses vital rhythm and balance.

The rawness and ugliness of modern European life is the sign of biological inferiority, of an insufficient or false relation to environment, which produces strain, wasted effort, revolt or failure. Just as a mechanistic industrial civilisation will seek to eliminate all waste movements in work, so as to make the operative the perfect complement of his machine, so a vital civilisation will cause every function and every act to partake of vital grace and beauty. To a great extent this is entirely instinctive, as in the grace of the old agricultural operations, ploughing, sowing and reaping, but it is also the goal of conscious effort in the great Oriental cultures – as in the calligraphy of the Moslem scribe, and the elaboration of Oriental social etiquette. Why is a stockbroker less beautiful than a Homeric warrior or an Egyptian priest? Because he is less incorporated with life, he is not inevitable, but accidental, almost parasitic. When a culture has proved its real needs, and organised its vital functions, every office becomes beautiful. So too with dress, the full Victorian panoply of top hat and frock coat undoubtedly expressed something essential in the 19th century culture, and hence it has spread with that culture all over the world as no fashion of clothing has ever done before. It is possible that our descendants will recognise in it a kind of grim and Assyrian beauty, fit emblem of the ruthless and great age that created it ; but, however that may be, it misses the direct and inevitable beauty that all clothing should have, because, like its parent-culture, it was out of touch with the life of nature and of human nature as well.

The essential need of our civilisation is a recovery of these lost contacts – a return to the sources of life. A hundred years ago Comte realised the dangers of European disintegration and the need for the recreation of a positive social order, based on the European Culture-tradition. Comte's view of civilisation was, however, strongly intellectualist. It was left for Leplay to analyse the ultimate human and natural bases of a society in the life of the region. Yet the two methods supplement one another since every society has two kinds of roots in place and time – in the natural life of the Region, and in the tradition of the Culture. However far the process of degeneration has gone, there is always a possibility of regeneration, if a society is conscious of this double bond through which it enters into communion, on the one hand with the life of nature, on the other with the life of humanity.

Christopher Dawson, 1923

5

CATHOLICISM AND ECONOMICS

NEVER in the world's history have economic problems played such a large part in human life or had such direct influence on human thought as at present. Economics have come to overshadow politics, to absorb into their sphere the entire social question. Even the man in the street has learnt that his personal welfare is intimately bound up with an economic system. He may be indifferent towards politics, sceptical of the value of philosophy and science, hostile towards religion, but in economic matters his interest and prejudices are keen. Hence the rise of Socialism—the success of an economic gospel and an economic interpretation of life. Hence too a new spirit of criticism towards religion, which is felt to be indifferent towards the things which are so vitally important—it is the 'opium of the poor' which drugs them into contentment with their lot, and indifference towards their true interest.

This excessive preoccupation with economic problems is, however, abnormal and temporary. A healthy society is no more troubled about its economic organisation than a healthy man is troubled about his digestion. The present unrest is a symptom of disease, as well as a symptom of necessary change. Modern society is traversing that critical period of its existence, which the Ancient World also went through during the century that preceded the Augustan Peace. In both cases the material resources of society have outstripped its moral control. It is the crucial moment in the life of a civilisation – a time when societies and individuals are beset by temptations to violent remedies and excessive hopes, alternating with apathy and despair. When the crisis is over, when society has either mastered its difficulties or accepted a compromise with them, human life again becomes normal; economic problems sink back into their proper perspective, and man's spiritual needs once more reassert themselves. After the Peace of Augustus comes the Gospel of Christ.

And so it is with our own problems. The present economic unrest is a side issue—though a side issue of vast importance—which distracts men's minds from the ultimate problems of life; it is this, not religion, which is the true 'opium of the poor.' Only when the present economic question is settled will the real opportunity of Catholicism come. The economic settlement affords the material preparation for the religious settlement, that is to say for the conversion of our civilisation.

Yet we are far from wishing to assert that Economics belong to a region apart from Religion. Religion, to be worthy of the name, must claim to be the inspiration of every side of human life, and the economic life, however exaggerated are the claims the Socialists make for it, is certainly one of the fundamental forces that have moulded the development of human society. Among primitive peoples the connection between religion and economics is clear enough. That by which man lives is holy: there is a mystery in all the processes by which the earth is brought to bear fruit for the support of man, and the one great end of sacrifice and spell and purification is to co-operate with the forces of nature in producing good harvests, numerous flocks, and favourable seasons.

In the case of Christianity, however, this is much less obvious. At first sight it would seem impossible to conceive of a religion more hostile to the economic view of life. It stands at the opposite pole to the nature religion, for it is essentially 'other-worldly' and bases its teaching on a new scale of values in which the old economic and natural values disappear, or are reversed. Nevertheless it will be seen that Christianity eventually reconquers the economic life for itself, by bringing that also into relation with spiritual values.

Part I: Catholic Principles and Economics

The Christian attitude towards wealth and the use of material goods is expressed in the two great evangelical ideals of Poverty and Charity. These are intimately connected with one another, for that are respectively the negative and positive aspect of the teaching of Jesus concerning the Kingdom of God. The present world and the natural order are but the preparation for the world to come – the spiritual and supernatural order. This alone is worthy of man's efforts, and the goods of the present world are only of value if they are used for spiritual ends. If they are treated as ends in themselves, they become evil.

'Be not solicitous, therefore, saying: What shall we eat; or What shall we drink; or Wherewithal shall we be clothed? For after all these things do the Gentiles seek. For your Father knoweth that you have need of all these things. Seek ye therefore the Kingdom of God, and his justice, and all these things shall be added unto you.' 'A man's life does not consist in the abundance of things that he possesses,' but in his 'riches towards God.' A superfluity of material wealth is really an obstacle to the attainment of the true end of life. Therefore our Lord counsels his followers to strip themselves of the unnecessary like an athlete before the race, or rather like a man in a sinking ship, who has more chance of safety the less he has on him. 'How hardly shall they that have riches enter the Kingdom of God.' Leave world cares to worldly men – the dead to the dead. 'Sell what you possess and give alms. Make for yourself bags that grow not old: a treasure in heaven that faileth not.'

All this insistence on the perils of wealth and the blessedness of poverty does not rest, as so many modern writers think, on a desire for social justice. Justice, as we shall see, has a very important place in Catholic doctrine, but it is not the foundation of the evangelical teaching about poverty. That is simply a consistent development of the new spiritual and otherworldly valuation of life, which was the work of Jesus, and as such it has inspired the attitude of the Catholic Church ever since, and has been the principle of the ascetic life and of the monastic institution. Alike to St. Anthony in the third century, and to St. Francis in the thirteenth, the words of our Lord, 'If thou wilt be perfect, sell all that thou hast, and give to the poor and come and follow me,' came as a personal command, and the life of St. Francis, so vital and yet so utterly independent of all that external goods can do to make life liable, is a standing sample of the way in which the Christian spirit transcends all economic categories and laws. Nor is the realisation of this ideal limited to Oriental or mediaeval society, in which a money economy hardly exists. During the very years when Adam Smith was working out his economic system, Benedict Joseph Labre, his junior by twenty-five years, as a wanderer and beggar on the highways of Europe, was disproving by his life the fundamental postulates of the new science.

This ideal of Holy Poverty and of the blessedness of the non-economic life is the negative side of the Gospel teaching. The same view of life finds its positive expression in the precept of Charity, which is the true inspiration of the Christian life in economics as well as in other matters. All that a man has, whether of external goods or of personal powers and opportunities, is given him not for his own enjoyment, but for the service of God and man. The man who uses his powers and his wealth for his own gratification is like the faithless slave in the parable who swills his master's wine and misuses the fellow-servants whose welfare has been entrusted to him. On the other hand, though wealth sought as an end in itself is an obstacle to the Kingdom of God, it is not without its value, if it is used as a vehicle of spiritual love. To feed the hungry, to clothe the naked, to care for the sick and the prisoner is as it were a personal service to the Son of Man Himself.

This is to 'make friends of the Mammon of Iniquity'—to convert material, indifferent things into spiritual goods—'riches towards God.' It is not that the Gospel treats the alleviating of economic distress as an end in itself, it is again, as in the teaching on voluntary poverty, a question of the spiritual revaluation of life.

Charity was to b e the controlling force in the brotherhood of the Kingdom of God, and if this spiritual force was real, it must show itself in all things from the highest to the lowest. 'Whether you eat or drink, or whatever you do, do all to the glory of God.' To the average man the economic life is the one side of life that really matters, and a religion that leaves this unaffected, as did English Evangelical Pietism a century ago, thereby shows itself to be unreal. Consequently the duty of almsgiving, the realisation in the economic sphere of the Christian fraternity, was the chief external activity of the early Church, and it was carried out on a scale that is difficult to realise in the present age, amounting, as it often did, to a real redistribution of property.

Yet in the charity of the early Church, from the 'communism' of the first believers at Jerusalem onwards, there was no attempt to secure an improvement of economic conditions as such. There was simply an indifference to wealth to external conditions generally, and a determination to conform the daily life of the faithful to the new laws of the spiritual world that had been revealed.

If the Christian had passed from death to life, from darkness to light, it was because he had received the Life of God, and that life was Love. It was impossible to possess that Life and not to love the brethren, and it was equally impossible to love the brethren without showing it in external things. As Christ has laid down His life for us, so we ought to lay down our life for the brethren, says St. John, and he goes on: 'He that has the substance of this world, and shall see his brother in need and shall shut up his bowels from him; how doth the Charity of God abide in him? My little children, let us not love in word nor in tongue, but in deed and in truth.'[23] This is the spirit of Catholic charity as opposed alike to external almsgiving and to modern social reform, which is a matter of results. It is the outward manifestation of a true living, personal force of love the spirit of St. Peter Claver or St. Vincent de Paul, rather than that of the Charity Organisation Society or of the Fabian Society.

But if these two great principles-indifference to external goods and brotherly love, are the foundations of the Catholic attitude towards economics, they are nevertheless not all-sufficing. Taken by themselves would suggest the complete segregation of Christians from the ordinary life of society, and they find their most complete realisation in the religious life – the state of perfection. If this state is held up, not as an ideal counsel, but as a law binding upon all Christians, we are led towards a social teaching which is not that of the Church, but that of the anarchic and 'spiritual'

---

[23] I John 3:16-18

sects which have always existed from the second century to the present day. All these, whether they look forward to a millennial Kingdom of the Saints as did the Montanists, the Anabaptists and the Fifth Monarchy Men, or whether they preach the perfect life like the Apostolics, the Fraticelli, the Catharists, or, in our own age, the followers of Tolstoy, agree in condemning the state, secular business and secular civilisation as radically and irremediably bad, and it is natural for them to condemn the institution of property, like marriage and civil authority, as an infringement of the spirit of their gospel.

But Catholicism cannot acquiesce in any such division of life, for it teaches an integration of the whole of life, so far as life is not dominated by perverse instincts of will. The God who redeems man is the same God who created him, and with him all exterior nature. It is the function of man to be the head of the material order, and to spiritualise inferior things by using them for God. Though the natural and the supernatural are two distinct orders, to which in a sense the secular and the religious lives correspond, yet both are directed to the same ultimate end. Thus economic life, though it is essentially a co-operation for the provision of material goods, is for the Christian a co-operation governed and inspired by love.

Its special rights and duties are subordinated to this ultimate and fundamental law – the New Law of Christ. This secular life, whether political or economic, cannot be withdrawn from its subordination to the spiritual life, nor can its laws be absolute laws as Ricardo and Bentham conceived them. The only distinction that the Church can recognise is that between counsel or perfection, and precept or obligation; she can never admit an absolute final distinction between the religious and the secular life, for both serve the same end and the lower is instrumental to the higher.

This conception of the unity of life is the true characteristic of the Christian civilisation which spiritualises and sanctifies the whole of life. It inspires all the achievements of the Middle Ages, the philosophy of St. Thomas, the poetry of Dante, the political and economic life of the free cities. We see it naively but impressively portrayed in the mediaeval frescoes in the Spanish Chapel of Sta. Maria Novella at Florence, in which all the estates of the Christian people are ranged in order, on the right hand the spiritual hierarchy of Pope and cardinals and bishops, abbots and monks and friars; on the left emperor and princes and nobles, merchants and craftsmen and peasants. Thus the whole Christian people is conceived as a great organic unity. Each order has its function, in the life of the whole; each has a necessary and God-given work to perform; each alike is bound by the law of duty, of work, of mutual service and love: one order does not exist for the sake of another, but all alike co-operate in their common service of God and His Church.

Now this is nothing else but the extension to the whole of life of the principles that St. Paul had laid down concerning supernatural things. For as the body is one and has many members, and all the members of the body, though they are many, yet are one body, so also is Christ... The eye cannot say to the hand: I do not need thy help, nor again the head to the feet: I have no need of you. Yea, much more those that seem to be the more feeble members of the body are more necessary... That there might be no schism in the body, but that the members might be mutually careful of one another.'[24]

This passage applies, it is true, only to the distribution of supernatural graces and offices within the Church: to St. Paul the state lay outside the Body of Christ in the darkness of this world; but when society as a whole had become Christian, it was natural that this image of the body and its members should be transferred to Christian society as a whole, as is done by St. Thomas Aquinas and other great mediaeval theologians.

According to their principles the economic functions exist as necessary parts of the social organism with their own rights and duties. Like the more honourable offices of rulers or judges, they must be discharged conscientiously and disinterestedly. Whether they are productive or distributive, they exist not for the sake of private gain, but for the public utility and the common good. For example, the profit of the merchant, St. Thomas teaches, should not be arbitrary or excessive, but should be the just payment for his labour in the services of the community.[25]

In the same way wealth and property must be governed by these principles. They are the fundamental mechanism of the economic life, and they exist in order to facilitate that co-operation for ultimate spiri-

---

[24] I Cor. 12:12, 21-22, 25

[25] *Summa Theologiae*, IIa-IIae. 77, a.4.

tual ends in which the life of a Christian society consists. The economic ideal is that every member of the society should have the material resources with which to live a good and complete human life, as the basis on which to build his spiritual life.

This does not mean that the economic position of every man should be the same. Their material resources must be adapted to the special functions that they are called upon to discharge. That is to say the peasant and the worker should have the property they need for their work, the merchant for his business and the ruler or the official for the discharge of his office. And all of them, in so far as they are called to the married state, should also have the means of establishing a household and sharing in the complete family which is the necessary basis of Christian society.

But if these are the ideals, it must be remembered that their actual realisation is strictly limited by material circumstances and environment. Practically all societies have lived under the pressure of want. Apart from recurrent periods of destruction and famine in which men struggle for bare existence, and 'the good life' goes to the wall, society as a whole has never enjoyed plenty: that has been, at best, the privilege of some favoured class. The social question is not only a question of the just distribution of property, it is also a question of the just distribution of privation, which has also been hitherto an inevitable concomitant of economic life. This is but little recognised by the majority of social reformers, who take the maximum of plenty that has hitherto been attained as an inevitable minimum, and the temporary prosperity of an over-industrialised society as the natural level of economic development.

There is, however, no doubt that an unfair distribution of wealth and privation is more often to be found in prosperous than in poor societies. It is the existence or creation of surplus wealth which fives to classes and individuals that overwhelming economic strength, which is so often abused; and in the pastoral tribe or the peasant community, which always lives on the hunger line, there is often less real misery than in a rich and highly-civilised community.

But granting these limitations, the problem of the attainment of the best possible distribution of wealth remains. How is this problem to be solved?

The modern sociologist would no doubt reply that this is the business of the State: that since economic functions exist for the service of the community, it is for the community to determine on their recompense. Catholic tradition has, however, unhesitatingly rejected this solution, and has favoured white a different view, one which may be described as the recognition of a natural or quasi-natural right of individual possession, and its subordination to the common good by the spirit of Christian love. Let us see how St. Thomas explains and defends this fundamental position. His teaching is representative not only of the Catholic thought of the Middle Ages, but also of the Catholic social movement of the nineteenth century.

The possession of exterior things, he says, is natural to man, for inferior things are ordained by God for the purpose of succouring man's needs. The division or appropriation of things is based on human law. It is not contrary to natural law, but is an addition to it devised by human reason. It is indeed necessary to human life for three reasons. First, because every man is more careful to procure what is for himself alone than that which is common to many or to all . . Secondly, because human affairs are conducted in a more orderly way, if each man is charged with taking care of some particular thing himself, whereas there would be confusion if everyone had to look after any one thing indeterminately. Thirdly, because a more peaceful state is ensured to man, if each one is contented with his own, for quarrels arise more often where there is no division of the thing possessed. *As regards the use* of external things, however, man ought to possess them not as his own, but as common, so that he is ready to communicate them to others in their need.

> For the division and appropriation of things which is based on human law do not preclude the fact that man's needs have to be remedied by some means of these very things. Hence whatever certain people have in superabundance is due, by natural law to the purpose of succouring the poor. For this reason St. Ambrose says: "It is the hungry man's bread that you withhold, the naked man's cloak that you store away, the money that you bury in the earth is the price of the needy man's redemption and freedom." Since however there are many who are in need, while it is impossible for all to be succoured by means of the same thing, each one is entrusted with the

stewardship of his own things, so that out of them he may come to the aid of those who are in need.[26]

But private property, even if it be a matter of human contrivance and instituted for the sake of common utility, is not on that account the creation of the State. The 'human law' of which St. Thomas speaks is not the enacted law of a sovereign. As Pope Leo XIII says in his famous encyclical, *Rerum novarum*, man has economic rights apart from, and prior to, his membership of the State. The right of property follows necessarily on the foundation of the family, which is 'a true society anterior to every kind of state and nation, and invested with rights and duties of its own, totally independent of the civil community.'

There is, moreover, an internal and necessary connection between the two fundamental principles, the duty of charity and the right of individual possession. To the Catholic, life is essentially a spiritual activity, and the economic life, instead of being the foundation and cause of all the rest, as Marx and Engels taught, or an independent sphere governed by its own absolute laws, as the classical economists maintained, is but the plastic material through which this spiritual activity may express itself.

Consequently an organisation of industry, however perfect in itself, in which the individual has no power over his own life and no opportunity for the free service of others, is no fit instrument for the realisation of the Catholic social ideal. The latter requires a certain sphere of economic liberty in which the individ-

---

[26] *Summa Theologiae*, IIa-IIae. 2.

ual can exercise his free will and find material for the realisation of his spiritual activities. Every man is the artist of his own life, and he needs his own materials, even in inferior things, if his creation is to be complete. Otherwise he becomes the mere instrument of another's purpose, whether it be the will of a despot or the group-purpose of a national mind.

It is the aim of the Christian life to make political and economic relations subordinate to the inward life: to convert them from a mechanism which enslaves into the free working of a personal and moral activity. The realisation of this end may appear an impracticable ideal, and so it is from the politician's point of view, which takes account of human nature alone; but to the Catholic who sees human nature restored and transformed by divine charity, all things are possible. The essential work of the Church in the world consists in bringing humanity into contact with this transforming divine force, so that from the inner centre of the individual soul outwards every human activity is affected and changed. This is the true social reform, and we have now to see how it has been carried out in the changing conditions of economic life during the past ages of the Church's history and what are the problems with which she is faced in that new world that is gradually coming into being.

Part II: The Application of Christian Principles to Economics in the Past.

The infant Church was born at a time when the greatest state that the world has ever seen was attaining to its full development. The whole civilised world west of the Euphrates was united under a single head. The age of civil war, of social unrest, of the exploitation of the conquered peoples was at last over. Everywhere new cities were springing up, trade was flourishing and population increasing. It was 'the hour of the prince of this world,' the apotheosis of triumphant material power and wealth.

And yet the whole splendid building rested on non-moral foundations-often on mere violence and cruelty. The divine Caesar might be a Caligula or a Nero, wealth was an excuse for debauchery and the prosperity of the wealthy classes was based on the institution of slavery – not the natural household slavery of primitive civilisation, but an organised plantation-slavery which left no room for any human relation between slave and master.

The early Church could not but b e conscious that she was separated by an infinite gulf from this great material order, that she could have no part in its prosperity or in its injustice. She was in this world as the seed of a new order, utterly subversive of all that had made the ancient world what it was. Yet though she inherited the spirit of the Jewish protest against the Gentile world-power, she did not look for any temporal change, much less did she attempt herself to bring about any social reform. The Christian accepted the Roman state as a God-given order appropriate to the condition of a world in slavery to spiritual darkness, and concentrated all his hopes on the return of Christ and the final victory of the supernatural order. Meanwhile he lived as a stranger in the midst of an alien world.

> While living in Greek and barbarian cities, according to each man's lot, and following the local customs in clothing and food and the rest of life, they show forth the wonderful and confessedly strange character of their own citizenship. They dwell in their own countries as though they were sojourners; they share all things as citizens and suffer all things as strangers. They marry and bear children, like the rest, but they do not expose their children. They have a common table, but not a common bed. They are in the flesh, but they do not live after the flesh. They pass their time on earth, but they live as citizens in heaven.[27]

Thus the Christians were held to be a 'Third Race'—*Tertium Genus*—standing apart alike from the Gentile and from the Jew, living a hidden life which had only an external and accidental connection with the life of the heathen world around them.

This withdrawal from social life, this passive acceptance of external things as matters of no consequence, seems at first sight to prove that Christianity had no direct influence on social and economic conditions. As a matter of fact, this attitude produced the most revolutionary consequences. Ancient society and the civic religion with which it was bound up centred in a privileged citizen class, and under Roman rule

---

[27] Epistle to Diognetus V

citizenship was directly based on economic status: that is to say a man's position in his own city and in the empire at large was determined by his property assessment under the census. There was a constant process of competition under the early empire, by which freedmen and tradesmen became landowners, landowners raised themselves to the curia of their city, and rich provincial decurions became Roman knights and even senators.

Christianity substituted membership of the Church for membership of the city as a man's fundamental and most important relationship to his fellows. In the new religious society rich and poor, bond and free, Roman citizen and foreigner, all met on an absolutely equal footing; Not only were these earthly distinctions overlooked, they were almost inverted, and it was the poor who were privileged and the rich who were humbled. This world was to the rich, but the new world—the only world that mattered—was above all the inheritance of the poor. 'Hath not God chosen the poor in this world, rich in faith, and heirs of the kingdom that God has promised to them that love Him?' says Saint James. 'But you have dishonoured the poor man' (if you have respect to persons). 'Do not the rich oppress you by might, and do not they drag you before the judgment seats? Do not they blaspheme the good name that is invoked upon you?'[28]

No external change was made in status and possession, apart from that involved in charity. Indeed

---

[28] James 2:5-7

the poor are expressly counselled not to seek riches, not to take part in that social competition for individual advancement which was going on all round them. But the personal factor is utterly altered. To Cato[29] the slave is a chattel, to be sold when it becomes old or sickly, it is purely an economic instrument, to whom even the practices of religion are forbidden – all that must be left to the master. St. Paul sends the runaway slave Onesimus back to his master to be received not now as a slave, but instead of a slave, a most dear brother, especially to me. But how more to thee, both in the flesh and in the Lord, much

This contrast is not an economic one. The old legal rights are the same in the one case as in the other, but, an inner revolution has been effected, which must necessarily produce in time a corresponding change in all external social and economic relationships.

But this external change was slow in coming. Christianity during the first two centuries spread chiefly among the classes that had least economic influence – independent craftsmen, shopkeepers, freedmen, household slaves and so forth.

It affected neither the ruling classes nor the lowest grades of slave labour, which were found, not so much in the great cities of the Levant, the cradle of Christianity, as in the mines and on the great agrarian estates of the western provinces. When Christianity finally established a position for itself among the educated and the wealthy, the great economic transforma-

---

[29] Cato, *De Re Rustica* II, 142, etc.

tion of the ancient world had already begun, and civilisation was henceforward engaged in a continual and desperate battle with barbaric invaders from without, and economic decline from within. The one great problem now was how to save as much as possible of the inheritance of the past, and there was no room for any economic development other than that which was imposed by the hard law of necessity. Even so, however, the social changes in the Christian Empire were by no means all for the worse. In place of a society of capitalists and financiers, where wealth was ultimately derived from usury and from the exploitation of slave labour, there grew up a hierarchic society of officials and nobles, in which each class and occupation became a fixed caste, each with its own privileges and its own obligations. Instead of the slaves of the ergastula and the chain-gang, the land was cultivated by servile or semi-servile peasants, who had acquired the right to a family life, and even to a certain amount of economic independence.

The greater part of these changes was undoubtedly due to economic and political causes – to the inherent tendency of the imperial organisation, to the Orientalisation of Graeco-Roman civilisation, and above all to the decline of the lesser cities and the return to agricultural self-sufficiency on the rural estates. Nevertheless, the influence of the Church imprinted a distinctively Christian character on the whole process. Her ideals were opposed to all the main features of the earlier imperial society – to the luxury of the rich the idleness and dissipation of the poor and the oppression of the slaves. In place of the classical contempt for manual labour and 'vile mechanic arts,' which was the inheritance of Hellenistic culture, she did all in her power to substitute the duty and the honour of work. 'Blush for sin alone,' says St. John Chrysostom, 'but glory in labour and handicraft. We are the disciples of One who has been nourished in the house of a carpenter, of Peter the fisherman and-John Paul the tentmaker. By work we drive away from our hearts evil thoughts, we are able to come to the aid of the poor, we cease to knock importunately at the doors of others, and we accomplish that word of the Lord: "It is better to give than to receive."'

At the same time the Church held trade in little honour, and condemned unhesitatingly the usury which was the foundation of so much of the prosperity of the upper classes of Roman society. The nobles whom she honoured were not the great financiers and independent aristocrats of the old type, but the conscientious bureaucrats and soldiers. who served the new ideal of divine authority, vested in an hereditary imperial house, men like Lausus, the Chamberlain, Pammachius, the Consul, and the Count Marcellinus.

But above all the influence of Christianity was shown in the protection of the weak in a time of universal suffering and want. From the earliest times the Church had exercised charity upon the most lavish scale, and when at last she had the power to influence the rich, the extent of Christian almsgiving became so great as to cause a real economic change in the distribution of property. We find the great Fathers, St. Basil, St. Ambrose, St. Jerome, St. Augustine, above all St. John Chrysostom insisting on the duty of almsgiving in language which is as disconcerting to modern ears as it no doubt was to the rich men who first heard it: 'What you give to the poor man,' says St. Ambrose, 'is not yours, but his. For what was given for the common use, you alone usurp. The earth is all men's and not the property of the rich... Therefore you are paying a debt, and not bestowing a gift.'[30] And St. Basil even more forcibly declares: 'He who strips a man of his garments is called a thief. Is not he who fails to clothe the naked when he could do so worth of the same title? It is the bread of the hungry that you hold, the clothing of the naked that you lock up in your cupboard.'[31]

And as a practical commentary on these exhortations we find representatives of the great senatorial families such as Pinianus and Melania selling their vast estates and distributing all to the poor. The enfranchisement of slaves was an essential part of this work of charity. At first the economic position of Christians rendered it almost impossible, although even poverty could not prevent the heroic charity which St. Clement describes in the First Epistle to the Corinthians (lv): 'Many among ourselves have given themselves up to bondage that they might ransom others. Many have delivered themselves to slavery and provided food for others with the price they received for themselves.'

But under the Christian Empire, enfranchisement on a large scale became common. Melania is said to

---

[30] St. Ambrose *on Naboth XII*

[31] St. Basil *Hom. in Lucam*

have freed 8,000 slaves in the year 406 alone, and it was usual to give not only freedom, but also the land or money, with which they might earn their living.

In addition to this the Church was everywhere the protector of the poor, the orphan and the criminal. The bishop was not only the administrator of the charity of the faithful, he also acquired a recognised position as the representative of all the oppressed classes, as their defender not only against the rich, but against the government and the tax-collector. How widely these activities extended may be seen, for example, in the correspondence of St. Basil and in the record of his work for the people of Cappadocia during the famine of 367-8. The Church was gradually becoming an economic as well as a moral power, and as the economic condition of the Roman world declined, her relative wealth and importance increased till she became, above all in the Western provinces of the Empire, the only social force which retained life and vigour.

In the centuries that followed the collapse of imperial authority in the West, it was the bishops and the monasteries that took up the Roman tradition and ensured the continuance of ancient civilisation. We see St. Gregory the Great working to save Italy from destruction, devoting himself to every material need, and organising the estates of the Church to save Rome from famine. Under his administration the wealth of the Church was literally the 'patrimony of the poor' and also the mainstay of the economic life of the whole community. Nevertheless, he had no idea of building up a new social order. The world seemed to be passing away, the end of all things seemed at hand, and in a dying world he laboured to alleviate the sufferings of the people because they were his children, not because he had any hopes of the future.

A positive Christian order was only possible after the centuries of destruction had done their work, but meanwhile the foundations were being laid. In so far as civilisation survived at all it was a Christian civilisation, kept alive in monasteries and disseminated by Irish and Saxon monks. The Church was the only settled order; outside, all was anarchy and flux. Instead of the Church being in the state as a weak, voluntary corporation in a universal secular order, it was the state, weak, fluid and barbarous that was in the universal Church; and a man's primary citizenship and primary obligations were towards the latter. There was no independent economic sphere left. Instead of absolute economic rights and relations, we find a system of personal relationships – lordship and fealty, commendation and enfeoffment. Money economy and all that it stands for had vanished entirely, and land had become the only important form of wealth. Even in this there was no absolute ownership, only limited rights – half economic, half political. The distinction between rich and poor had given place to that between strong and weak. A man's social position depended not on his financial resources so much as on his fighting power, the number of retainers that he could muster and the extent of the lands that he could protect or ravage. In this simplified society the moral factor becomes all-important. A man of position could not be non-social or individualistic. He had to be either an oppressor or a defender of his subjects – a curse or a blessing to society. Even the contract between a man and his lord, which was the chief social bond, was not a mere matter of self-interest, like an economic contract, it involved personal loyalty and even devotion.

* * * * * * *

Thus it came about that the new social activity, which developed in the eleventh century, bore fruit in a Christian social order. The unity of Christendom, which had been a religious reality in the dark ages, now became also a great social and cultural reality. The Church was the ultimate social fact to which all local societies were bound to accommodate themselves. The Pope was the arbiter of Europe in all matters which involved a moral issue – questions of peace and war, of misgovernment or of the violation of individual and communal rights. His law—the Canon Law—was regarded by all as having precedence in social and economic matters, as well as in purely religious ones.

Thus when men of every class inspired by the new communal spirit began to form associations, confraternities and guilds, communes and sworn leagues of peace, all these had their basis and sanction in religion. It is often difficult to draw the line between the religious and the economic functions. For instance, in the case of the 'Charity of St. Christopher' at Tournai, we find a guild of merchants, which undoubtedly originated as a religious confraternity, but which had come in time to be charged with the whole administration of the city finances.

This religious character was equally clearly revealed in the case of these communes and leagues of peace, which were in opposition to the established order of feudal society, such is the great confraternity of the Capuchonnés which waged war on the brigands and nobles of Central France in 1182-3, and which was founded by a carpenter of Le Puy in obedience, as he declared, to the commands of Our Lady in a vision. The same energy that produced the Crusades was at work also in these little-known social movements which did so much to transform the life of Europe in the twelfth and thirteenth centuries.

When the mediaeval economic development was completed, every economic and social function possessed its corporate organisation, and the mediaeval city became a federation of self-governing societies, each of which had its own statutes, its own meeting place and chapel and its special patron saint. It is true that there was rivalry enough between the different classes and factions in the cities, between the aristocracy of merchants and the democracy of craftsmen, but nevertheless the economic theories of the theologians and the canonists were implicitly accepted by al parties as the foundations of industrial and commercial life. They taught that the economic order must be dominated not by the shifting forces of competition and self-interest, but by a fixed law of justice. Every individual and every corporation had their special offices to fulfil in the Commonwealth, and each was entitled to a just reward. The non-economic functions, whether political or religious, had their fiefs or benefices to enable them to fulfil their office. The economic occupations, though they also might possess their corporate endowments, were supported primarily by the sale of the products of their labour. The 'just price' was that which was a true recompense for the labour expended, whereas a price which was raised owing to scarcity and the need of the buyer, or lowered owing to the economic weakness of the seller, was unjust and illegitimate.

The most honourable economic functions were those that were most productive; hence the mediaeval preference for the husbandman and the craftsman to the merchant. The true end of labour was not pecuniary profit, but rather the service of others. To work for profit alone, was to turn honest work into usury,[32] and all occupations which looked for excessive profit, or in which the profit was unrelated to the expenditure of labour, were looked on with disfavour. Mediaeval life and literature are full of this ideal of disinterested labour. We see it in Piers Plowman, and in the Plowman of Chaucer, who 'woulde thrash and thereto dike and delve, For Christe's sake, for every poore wight, Withouten hire, if it lay in his might,' and the Church has raised it to her altars in the person of St. Isidore Agricola.

The ideal for craftsmen was no less high. 'It is good and true work,' says a mediaeval writer, 'when craftsmen by the skill and cunning of their hands in beautiful buildings and sculptures spread the glory of

---

[32] Cf. Jansen, *History of the German People*, Vol. II, p. 9

God, and make men gentle in their spirits, so that they find delight in all beautiful things, and look reverently on all art and handicraft, as a gift of God for the use, enjoyment, and edification of mankind.'[33]

These theories and ideals found their practical expressions in the economic regulations of the cities and the guilds.

Membership of the latter was compulsory, so that each guild possessed a monopoly of its own craft. It represented the principle of corporate responsibility, both towards the community by guaranteeing the quality of the wares produced, and towards its members by ensuring to all equal opportunity and mutual assistance in need.

The city, for its part, aimed at safeguarding the supply of necessaries at a just price. All goods had to be sold by retail in the open market, and numerous laws against 'engrossing, forestalling, and regrating,' were directed against any attempts on the part of individuals or rings to dominate the market, or to control supply. This was looked on in the Middle Ages as the essential function of the state in economic matters.[34]

---

[33] Jansen, *Hist. of the German People*, Vol. II, p. 97.

[34] Professor Ashley thus sums up the general tendency of mediaeval economic legislation: 'Doubtless the yardlings and cotters and craftsmen sometimes suffered from famines; doubtless their surroundings were often unsanitary. Still, there was a standard of comfort which general opinion recognised as suitable for them, and which prices were regulated to maintain. But now we are content that wages should be determined by the standard of comfort which a class can manage to maintain, left to itself, or rather exposed to the competition of machinery and immigrant foreign labour' (*English Economic History*, Vol. I, p. 139).

Outside the towns these co-operative economic ideals had less scope, for feudal society always rested to a great extent on the rule of force. But even there the same tendencies were at work. The influence of the Church tended to transform the right of the stronger into an office of honour and service in the Christian commonwealth. As mediaeval royalty was consecrated into a semi-religious function, so too the military ruling class was spiritualised by the ideals of Christian knighthood into an order for the maintenance of justice and the defence of the weak and the oppressed.

Moreover, throughout the Middle Ages, the agricultural population made steady progress in communal rights and economic independence, and this in spite of the failure of their attempts (as in 1381) to shake off the feudal yoke altogether. By the fifteenth century their condition in most countries was even superior to that of the organised craftsmen of the free cities, as is shown, for instance, by the parish churches and guild chantries of rural England.

* * * * * * *

Unfortunately at the very time when the economic life of Europe was becoming strong enough to overcome the anarchy of feudal militarism the unity of Catholic Europe, on which mediaeval civilisation had rested, was passing away, and in its place there were arising the great national unitary states, each of which was organised against its neighbour as a complete social and economic whole. And while, on the one hand, these did away with the ideal unity of Christendom, on the other they replaced the practical social unit – the city. For it is important t o remember that the 'state' (*civitas*), which was charged with the regulation of economic matters both in medieval practice and in the theory of the moral theologians, was, not the sovereign state that we know, but the mediaeval city, itself a part of the larger unity of province or kingdom, which in its turn was but a member of the whole Christian commonwealth.

In the new state the co-operative principle was replaced by the absolute theories of the Renaissance lawyers and statesmen. Where communal liberties were not destroyed, they became converted into class privileges,[35] the rights of free association vanished, and in Protestant lands a new wealthy class grew far on the plunder of the abbeys, and the partial confiscation of the common land. It is true that the old principle of economic regulation for moral and social ends did survive, but it was controlled by the King's Council in the interests of the state, and was no longer related to the common social good of the Christian commonwealth.

In some cases this control was exercised in a really Christian spirit. Indeed the Spanish colonial legislation with respect to the Indians, and the early French government of Canada are perhaps the most remarkable instances in history of the control of economic

---

[35] In Southern Europe the more or less decadent guilds were destroyed mainly by the 'enlightened despotism' of the eighteenth century, e.g. by Leopold in Tuscany and by Charles IV in Spain. In both these cases their suppression went hand in hand with that of the popular religious confraternities.

interests by Christian ideals of justice. The colonial policy of Holland and England, however, was inspired by a very different spirit, and even the Puritan colonists of New England showed an almost complete disregard of the rights of the aborigines. The record of the English in the West Indies was of course infinitely worse.[36]

Meanwhile two spiritual forces were preparing the way for drastic changes in economic theory and social life: these were Protestant Individualism and Philosophic Rationalism. Ever since the Reformation, Protestantism had shown a strong tendency to develop an economic mentality of its own. Calvin himself had been the first to break completely with the Catholic tradition regarding usury, and his followers, who combined moral rigourism with individualism, regarded economic success as a sign of God's favour towards the industry of the saints and

---

[36] Cf. 'On Spain' in *Cambridge Modern History*, Vol. X, ch. 8, esp. p. 263, etc. 'On France and the contrast of French and English systems,' ditto Vol. VII, pp. 97-102.

insisted far more on the sinfulness of idleness than on the duty of charity.[37]

In the lands where these ideals had free play – Holland, Great Britain, above all New England, a new type of character was produced, canny, methodical and laborious; men who lived not for enjoyment but for work, who spent little and gained much, and who looked on themselves as unfaithful stewards before God, if they neglected any opportunity of honest gain.

---

[37] 'While there was a strong sends (among Puritans) of the religious duty of insisting on hard and regular work for the welfare, temporal and eternal, of the people themselves, there was complete indifference to the need of laying down or enforcing any restrictions as to the employment of money. Capital was much needed in England, and still more in Scotland, for developing the resources of the country and for starting new enterprises; freedom for the formation and investment of capital seemed to the thoughtful city men of the seventeenth century, who were mostly in sympathy with Puritanism, the best remedy for the existing social evils. They were eager to get rid of the restrictions imposed by the Pope's laws, which it was still possible to bring up in the ecclesiastical courts, as well as to be free from the efforts of the King's Council to bring home to the employing and mercantile classes their duty to the community... In so far as a stricter ecclesiastical discipline was aimed at, or introduced, it had regard to recreation and to immorality of other kinds, but was at no pains to interfere to check the action of the capitalist or to protect the labourer.' Quoted by Tröltsch Soziallehre and W. Cunningham, *The Moral Witness of the Church on the Investment of Money and the use of Wealth*, 711-712. He also gives examples of the Scotch legislation against unemployment (1663). 'Capitalists who set up manufactories were empowered to impress any vagrants, and "employ them for their service, as they see fit," for eleven years without wages except meal and clothing. Good subjects were recommended to take into their service poor and indigent children, who were to do any task assigned to them till they had attained the age of thirty, and to be "subject to their master's correction and chastisement in all manner of punishment (life and torture excepted)".' Compare the system of binding parish apprentices to the manufacturers in England from 1760-1816.

On the other hand, the philosophers of the eighteenth century advocated the abolition of economic restrictions on abstract grounds. They taught that there existed a law of nature which man had only to follow in order to attain happiness. Self-interest and the desire for pleasure were divinely-implanted instincts which made for the common good, since the advantage of the individual and that of society were naturally and providentially co-ordinated.

These theories were everywhere dominant among the ruling classes in the eighteenth century, and when they were fused with the Protestant Individualism of the mercantile classes of Great Britain they produced the new economic philosophy of Adam Smith, the father of classical political economy.

The new conditions of international trade and, above all, the technical discoveries that revolutionised eighteenth century industry, provided an opportunity for putting the new principles into practice. Instead of gradually rebuilding a national system of trade and industry suited to the new conditions, the statesmen and publicists, who had embraced the new ideas, abandoned all ideas of regulating economic forces. They believed that the true interests of society were safest in the hands of those who had most to lose or gain. Consequently alike in the new industry with regard to wages and conditions of labour, and in the new agriculture with regard to enclosures, the interests of the mass of the people were absolutely subordinated to those of the possessing and employing classes.

Undoubtedly industrialism throve under this regime, and England became the workshop of the world, far outstripping the more conservative continental countries, but so far from producing the freedom and prosperity of all classes as the theorists had promised, a most disastrous effect was produced on the standard of living of the workers. Society was brought into a state of dependence on material and non-moral factors such as had not existed since the days of the slave dealers and publicans of the later Roman Republic. By the end o f the century it had become impossible for the economists to shut their eyes to the evils of the new system. Instead of modifying their principle, however, they adopted a pessimistic fatalism, a belief in the existence of unalterable economic laws governing the rate of wage and standard of life of the working classes, which rendered all attempts towards an improvement of conditions, whether by private charity, state intervention or trade union organisation, worse than useless. The only remedy that the economists could suggest for the misery produced by the new industrialism was the limitation of the wage-earning population, and though this was advocated by a few writers, such as Malthus, Bentham and Place, the majority surrendered completely to economic fatalism, and refused any hope to the poor, save the purely individual one of pushing and thrusting a way out of the ranks of the workers into the middle classes – the gospel of self-help.

Thus there arose the complete anti-Christian economic theory, according to which the one duty of the rich was to increase their wealth, while the labour of the poor was a tool, to be bought in the market as cheaply as possible. Man's economic life was not regulated by moral laws, nor could it be transformed by charity; it was a region apart, dominated solely by the laws of supply and demand, by the increase of population and of capital.

These laws were accepted as unquestionable axioms by the majority of philosophers and politicians. They met with resistance only in the uninstructed conscience of the people. Nothing is more remarkable than the way in which the poor clung almost instinctively to the old Christian principles, of the just price and the just wage, of the right of the craftsman to live by his craft, and the duty of society to regulate economic conditions according to moral ends. But apart from the case of Cobbett, in whom this suppressed medievalism found vehement expression, the workers remained almost leaderless. Their innate conservatism was shocked alike by the wild porto-Socialism of Spence and Hodgskin and Gray, and by the scientific Benthamite Radicalism of Francis Place, while the middle class reformers whom they supported used their new power to pass the new Poor Law and to vote against the Factory Bills of Sadler and Shaftesbury.

During this first period of industrialism, Catholic opinion was hardly touched. The new system was almost entirely confined to Protestant countries. Only in Ireland, and there chiefly after the famine, did the new doctrine of the rights of ownership come into open collision with the mind of a Catholic society.

On the continent, the Church was still engaged in her great struggle with the principles of the Revolution, and it was only after the old political order had finally passed away that industrialism really commenced in Catholic Europe.[38] It was not until 1848 that Baron von Ketteler, afterwards Bishop of Mainz (1850), first began to attack the new problems from the Catholic standpoint.

By the time that the continent had become industrialised on a scale at all comparable with that of Great Britain, the old fallacies of unrestricted individualism and unmodifiable economic laws had become largely discredited. From 1870 onwards we see the Great State, organising itself as an economic whole, in order to conquer its share in the world market.

But although the State now intervened to protect labour from the worst forms of exploitation, no change was made in the underlying principles of economic materialism. The non-moral struggle for gain was merely extended from the competition of individuals to the rivalry of great nations in the international markets – a rivalry which grew more and more desperate as the development of industry grew more intense. During the last fifty years there has been a progress in wealth and population such as the world had never seen before. Tee whole world has

---

[38] Nevertheless, the chief defender of the Catholic social tradition at the beginning of the nineteenth century, Louis de Bonald (1754–1840) insisted strongly on the falsity of the moral premises on which the new economic theories rested. Moreover, he advocated the restoration of the Guilds; the destruction of which he held to be one of the great evils resulting from the anti-Christian propaganda of the eighteenth century (Cf. *Legislation Primitive*, Pt. 3, ch. 4).

been drawn into one economic net. Prices and profits have become internationalised. The cheap labour and mass production of the industrial countries have been based, on the one hand, on the prairie-farming and cheap food of the new lands; on the other, on the control of the markets of India and other lands which were not yet industrialised.

All this was not, as the old economists thought, the fruit of economic freedom. The true note of that age was not economic liberty, but economic imperialism and exploitation, Great Britain, and after her the other countries of Western Europe, had used their monopoly of economic power to the full, and for a time it seemed that there would be no end to the progress of wealth and population, but in reality this development carried within it the seeds of its own destruction. Under the new conditions, the world was becoming too small for the gigantic development of the new industrial powers. In the scramble for markets and colonies they were driven to try and cut each other's throats. For the capacity of industrial mass-production is almost infinite, whereas the industrial markets are relatively restricted, owing to the fact that industrialism has become world-wide. In the new countries overseas, industrialisation has begun to outstrip agrarian development, and even the most backward countries are beginning to manufacture for themselves. Already we can see the same forces that drove Germany to her desperate venture at work in Japan; and what will happen when China begins to take a part in international trade proportionate to the numbers and industry of her population?

Moreover, a variety of causes co-operate to raise the cost and limit the supply of raw materials and of metals, and coal and oil; of cotton and wool; above all of food. We are beginning once again to face the great problem of the ancient world – the pressure of population on territory and food supply. Although the present world shortage is premature, it can only be a question of time before all the great countries of the world absorb their own food supply and manufacture for their own needs – as is almost the case with the United States at present. International trade will then consist, not as at present in the exchange of primary necessaries, but in highly specialised articles, and in tropical produce.

The coming of these conditions marks the beginning of that Stationary State, of which J. S. Mill wrote, an event as epoch-making in the history of the modern world as was the institution of the Roman Empire for antiquity.

It involves the ending of the last traces of laissez-faire, and a conscious regulation of the whole economic system, and the complete coordination of the latter with the other sides of the life of society.

Part III: The Economic Problem of the Present Age.

The establishment of such an economic order s demanded not only by external circumstances but also by human need.

In almost all the industrial countries the wage labourer is thoroughly disaffected. For almost a century he has been fed on the doctrines of political liberalism. He has been taught to believe in democracy, in the equal citizenship of all, and it is not surprising that he should have come at last to demand the application of these theories to his daily life – that is to economic matters. Hence the determination of organised labour to acquire a fixed standard of life, secure from the fluctuations of the international market. Hence too its tendency to look for the satisfaction of these ideals to Socialism, which had its birth at the time when the prospects of the working classes seemed most desperate, and which has shown itself ready to step into the place of the old governments in the political disintegration of Europe that has followed the world war.

The Socialist doctrines, especially in their 'Scientific' Marxian form, in spite of being a conscious revolt against the prevailing economic theories, nevertheless took over from the older economists their materialistic outlook and their faith in the operation of unmodifiable economic laws. They simply added to these fundamental conceptions a theory of historical evolution, by which they taught that the capitalist system was a necessary stage in the development of the individual handicrafts of the past into the scientific socialised industrialism of the future. As the capitalist manufacturer absorbs the multiple activities of the free craftsman, and subordinates them to a common task, so he too will be absorbed in turn by the final socialisation of industry, which is the end to which he is unconsciously tending. Thus Socialism is to Capitalism, what the modern factory was to the domestic workshop. Industry becomes ever more organised, capital continues to accumulate, until at last the State steps into the place of the trust and the millionaire, and takes control of the machinery that has grown too vast and complicated for private management.

This theory undoubtedly contains an element of truth. Marx was the first economist to realise the essentially transitory character of nineteenth century industrialism. His error lies in his conclusion – the necessity of State Communism. This means that the whole of life will be controlled by a single organism, which must be centralised, because, according to his theory, that is the inevitable tendency of the economic process, and which must be secularist in character and aims, in order to square with his materialist interpretation of history. This must infallibly produce an unbearable bureaucratic despotism; for if Communism is in any case (even in the tribe or the city) difficult to reconcile with personal freedom, what will it be when the communist society is a great centralised state, with all the traditions of national sovereignty behind it?

It will be said, no doubt, that in this, Socialism has merely recognised actual facts. We have the Great State already with its bureaucratic control over the life of the individual. All that Socialism does is to render this control more just and rational by destroying the anomaly of class distinction and economic privilege.

But Catholic social theory is far from approving of the Great State in either of its forms. The ideal that would secure at once a high profit for the British investor and a high standard of life for the British workman by the scientific exploitation of a vast tropical empire and which would use the economic strength thus gained to destroy the competition of its weaker rivals, is essentially un-Christian and shares in many of the objections that a Catholic can bring against the Socialist State. As Cardinal Dubois, of Paris, recently said, 'L'Etatisme est une heresie.'

The modern State, as we know it, is but a partial unity: it does not embrace either the whole of mankind, or the whole life of the individual man who belongs to it. It requires to be supplemented on the one hand by a spiritual society, on the other by national communities like itself. For as the ancient State was a city in a common civilisation of cities, so the modern State is a Nation in a society of Nations. There is a constant tendency for the State to make of itself an absolute unity and a final end. Mediaeval civilisation alone has succeeded in holding the balance between the claims of the whole and those of the parts, amongst which the National State is to be numbered. No partial unity has the right to arrogate to itself the position of final end, no society has the right to exclude all other societies.

And as there are societies above and outside the State, so too there are societies within and below it.

The State cannot deny the inherent right of its members to form other associations for special economic and social objects. To do so would be, in the words of Leo XIII, to contradict the very principle of its own existence, since it is the natural right of man to form these lesser societies, as well as the greater ones. Only by free association can m e n attain to a fully developed social and economic life. Consequently the true social ideal will not be found in the centralised unitary State which absorbs the entire control of the social and economic life of its members, but rather in the co-operative, federated State which gives free play to the activities of the individuals and the associations within it.

It is on these lines that the economic problem of our age must be solved, if the solution is to be in harmony with the needs of human nature and with Catholic principles. Economic life, as one of man's many activities, must find its own social expression and form its own organs. It must be ordered by the free association of individuals, not by a compulsory organisation proceeding from the centre of political authority.

The apologist for the present order would perhaps claim that it fulfils these conditions – that the capitalist system is simply the result of free economic association. Clearly the co-operative element is not altogether absent, for all economic life implies operation of some kind. 'Division of Labour' is really co-operation of labour, and international trade involves co-operation, as well as competition. But this co-operation may be servile or forced. The great works of the ancient world, such as the building of the pyramids, or the Great Wall of China, were performed by the labour of forced levies under the control of political or military authority; and it is the same with the great enterprises of the capitalist age, the Suez and Panama Canals for example. There is free co-operation among the directing elements, but the actual labourers are mere instruments.

In a settled industrial society, it is true, the wage labourers do possess their own organisations, but these are not organisations for production, they exist in order to defend the interests of the worker against the employer. Thus we find two free associations, the Trades Union and the Joint Stock Company, organised one against the other, and production necessarily suffers from the opposed interests and different policies of the two. The great problem of the present age is how to substitute a free co-operation for the jarring relations that at present subsist between the two. The capitalist solution, which still obtains to a great extent in the United States, is to eliminate the Trades Union and to trust the fortunes of the worker to the benevolent despotism of his employer, but that is obviously a reaction towards the servile non-co-operative economic relation.

On the other hand, the Socialist solution is to eliminate the capitalist by substituting the State or its agents for the Joint Stock Company, a solution which we have just criticised on the ground that it also is irreconcilable with freedom. The remains a third solution, which is purely co-operative. It is to amalgamate the two associations – that of the owners and that of the workers, so as to produce a single autonomous association, controlled and owned in equal shares by its actual working members.[39] This is the solution which has perhaps attracted independent thinkers more than any other. It was the ideal of Owen, of Fourier, of Lasalle, of Bishop Ketteler, of John Stuart Mill. The latter wrote in the later editions of his *Political Economy*:

> 'The form of association which, if mankind continue to improve, must be expected in the end to predominate, is not that which can exist between a capitalist as chief and workpeople without a voice in the management, but the association of the labourers themselves on terms of equality, collectively owning the capital with which they carry on their operations, and working under managers elected and removable by themselves.'[40]

It is scarcely possible to rate too highly the material benefits resulting from this,

> 'but this is as nothing compared with the moral revolution in society which would accompany it: the healing of the standing feud between Capital and Labour; the transformation of human life, from a conflict of classes struggling for opposite interests, to a friendly rivalry in the pursuit of a good common to all; the elevation of the dignity of Labour; a new sense of security and independence in the labouring class; and the conversion of each

---

[39] There is also a fourth solution, Guild Socialism, according to which the means of production are owned by the State, but are administered by the organised industrial unions or guilds. I have not discussed this separately, since it is essentially a compromise representing the reaction of Socialists to co-operative ideals. Some Guild Socialists remain in fact true Socialists, others, like Mr. A. Penty, appear to be pure co-operativists.

[40] *Op. cit.* 772-3 (ed. Ashley, 1909).

human being's daily occupation into a school of the social sympathies and the practical intelligence.'[41]

But these hopes, which were entertained by so many leaders of thought in the middle of the last century, were not destined to speedy realisation. During the next generation, the ideal of co-operative production became discredited alike among Socialists and individualists, It was an age of triumphant material progress, and men realised the difficulty of making piece-meal changes in the vast world organism of capitalist industry. It was hard to believe that a successful large scale industry could be built up on the savings of the workers, as J. S. Mill and the English Co-operators had hoped, and the alternative syndicalist plan of a revolution by violence and the forcible appropriation of capital must, apart from all questions of morality, so dislocate the fabric of society, as to imperil any kind of production.

Bishop Ketteler at least had fully realised the diffculties that lay in the way of this fundamental change, but he took long views and he could afford not to despair, since his ultimate hope rested on a force outside society.

> 'Every time that I have considered the situation,' he said in 1864, 'I have felt arise in me the hope and the certainty that the powerful aspirations of Christianity will take hold of this idea (of productive associations), and will realise it on a large scale. What an influence would not be exerted by the creation of societies of production based on Christian principles, in the midst of the territo-

---

[41] Ibid. 789-790.

ries of the white slaves of industrialism? What would not be the results, if men of good will, after assembling the necessary capital, offered the workers the chance of participating in a co-operative enterprise, in which all the profits which were not needed for the actual running of the business became the property of the workers themselves?

> Far be it from me to think that the working classes will suddenly and universally be succoured by these means. At present the only class in society that can act efficaciously—the class of the capitalists and industrial magnates—is far, far removed from Christianity. But no task is too great for that fire of divine charity which was brought into the world by Jesus Christ. There lies my hope for the future. Every fresh shipwreck of human efforts towards the help of the working classes only brings us nearer to the time when God Himself will come to their aid, through Christianity.'[42]

This is the spirit which 'believers all things, and hopeth all things,' but from any other standpoint it must be admitted that a co-operative organisation of industry was hardly possible under nineteenth century conditions. In these transitional periods, when conditions are constantly changing and the markets are expanding rapidly, the concentration of economic power in a few hands is inevitable. Under the new conditions that we have been discussing, however, the case is altered. The more the world is filled up and the main sources of production are allocated to the needs of particular countries, the more will the methods of production and the demands of consumers tend to

---

[42] Goyau 'Ketteler,' pp. 203-210. This important passage from *Die Arbeiter-Frage und das Christenthum* is unfortunately too long to quote in full.

become standardised, and the easier will it be for industry to reckon on a fixed output of a definite quality. During the last century the conquest of fresh markets, the introduction of new processes and the continual alterations in demand and supply, introduced an enormous element of risk, and favoured competition and speculation. But the industrial situation of the Stationary State will rather resemble that of the mediaeval city, where there was but little fluctuation in the quantity and quality of production and consumption.

Above all it must be remembered that under the new conditions the artificial isolation of industry from agriculture will have to come to an end. Hitherto social reformers have done little to co-ordinate the two. The Socialist generally wishes to conform all production to the model of large-scale industry. The individualism of the peasant shocks him just as much as the capitalism of the landlord, and he is ready to solve the agrarian problems by such drastic and unpractical measures, as the wholesale cultivation of the land by labour armies.[43]

On the other hand the agrarian reformer, who is anxious to improve conditions in his own department by the introduction of co-operative methods, is often hostile to the claims of the industrial population, and is inclined to leave the great cities and their problems to stew in their own juice. Hence the present violent opposition between town and country in Southern

---

[43] This was advocated by Marx and Engels in the Communist Manifesto and also, I believe, by Mr. Sidney Webb in the Minority Report of the Poor Law Commission. The latter proposed to utilise the unemployable and industrially inefficient class in this way!

Germany, Hungary, and to some extent in France, an opposition which is only not apparent in England on account of the relative unimportance of agriculture, and the fact that under the English system, the position of Labour has been worse in agriculture than in industry.

Hitherto the success of industrialism has been partly produced by the exploitation of the agrarian side of national life. For generations the strongest and most enterprising elements in the agricultural population have been drawn into the cities, and the country has been left to stagnate. But under the new conditions no country can afford to neglect its rural life. The prosperity of a society will come to be based more and more on its agricultural population and production; and industry, instead of being mainly dependent on international factors, will be the superstructure built upon that agrarian development. Thus it would once again be possible for there to be a real social bond between the city and the region in which it is placed, so that the former should be, not a secondhand product of cosmopolitan culture, but the civic expression of the local society. That is, of course, impossible in the case of the great industrial cities of the present day, but it is the ideal of the cooperative state to abolish this one-sided industrialism-to attain a balance between town and country, such as we now find only in the less industrialised countries, such as Denmark, Sweden, Holland and some parts of south Germany; and the realisation of this ideal is favoured by the new trend of economic conditions.

Catholic social policy in the past has shown a true instinct in its endeavours to preserve this balance by favouring the development of an independent peasant class, as in Ireland and South Germany, and by forwarding the co-operative movement among the rural population.[44] But it is equally in accordance with Catholic interests and ideals, though its attainment may be more difficult, for industry to be based on an independent, secure and prosperous artisan class, as for agriculture to be based on a free and prosperous peasantry. Only when both these tasks have been accomplished will the anarchy and greed, that are draining away the vital forces of our civilisation, be overcome, and the way made clear for the establishment of a Christian order.

Whatever happens to the modern world, the Church will continue to exist, and her work must be carried on even in a society that is externally heathenised. The great Catholic principles—Charity, Justice and Self-Denial—lie on a deeper plane than that of any economic programme or theory, and it is in the diffusion of these spiritual forces that the great duty of Catholics towards the modern world consists. Only through the Spirit of Christ can men learn to face these material problems i n a spiritual way-with love instead of selfishness, and with justice instead of prejudice. Spiritual darkness generates hatred and injustice, so that societies, like individuals, 'know not whither they go, because the darkness has blinded their eyes.' Material changes can bring no real healing

---

[44] *Cf.* Fr. Plater, *The Priest and Social Action.*

to mankind, unless they are rooted in a spiritual change — on that spiritual re-birth, which the modern world needs no less deeply, and seeks no less blindly than did the Mediterranean world two thousand years ago.

Christopher Dawson, 1924

6

CHRISTIANITY AND THE IDEA OF PROGRESS

FOR almost two centuries the idea of Progress has dominated the mind of Europe. It has passed from the philosopher to the politician and the man in the street, and has become so much the settled creed of our whole society that any attempt to question it is viewed either as a paradox or a heresy. It is true that the years since the war have been marked, especially on the Continent, by a wave of doubt and pessimism, nevertheless the belief in Progress is still dominant, and so deeply has it entered into our mentality that we find it hard to realise how recent and how limited has been its acceptance.

Yet when we look at the history of other ages and other civilisations we find a complete absence of any such conception. To the vast majority of the human race change has always seemed evil, and the Age of Gold lies in the distant past. The familiar lines of Horace—

Aetas parentum peior avis tulit
nos nequiores mox daturos
progeniem vitiosorem

express a sentiment that is as old as humanity, and which we can hear today on the lips of any elderly peasant. And this attitude is not confined to the unsophisticated type, which follows unthinkingly the traditions of a primitive way of life; it is far more strongly marked in the peoples of advanced culture. The higher the achievement of a civilisation, the greater is the measure of its disillusionment.

The great civilisations of the past have tended not merely to deny Progress, but to deny life itself. To the thinkers of ancient India, sensible existence and the whole temporal process is a web of illusion, which man must break through if he is to escape the growing accumulation of inherited ill. And the same pessimism may be traced more than a thousand years earlier in the ancient literature of Egypt and Babylonia.

"Death is before me today," writes an Egyptian poet of the third millennium B.C., "like a sick man going forth into a garden after his illness.

"Death is before me today, like the smell of myrrh, like sitting in the shade of the sail of a boat on a breezy day. Death is before me today, like the longing of a man to see his home, after many years' captivity."

If there is any civilisation other than our own in which we might expect to find the idea of Progress dominant, it is surely that of ancient Greece, for the Greeks seem to have possessed all the necessary foundations for such a belief.

Nowhere else in the history of the world was the actual advance of culture more rapid and triumphant; nowhere else has man had so clear a perception of the value of life and the possibilities of full development.

Hellenism is, in fact, the source of all the subsequent achievements of our European culture. It was the great creative force in art, literature, in science and philosophy, and the rise of modern European thought from the sixteenth century onwards was based directly on the recovery of the Hellenic heritage. Yet in this great heritage the idea of Progress has no place. It appears, early in the eighteenth century, as a spontaneous creation of the modern mind without any obvious links with the earlier development of European thought.

Not that the Greeks ignored it altogether. There is a long passage in the fifth book of Lucretius, no doubt derived in some measure from older Hellenic sources, which describes the progress of humanity under the stimulus of the struggle for existence from the purely animal conditions of its origin up to the highest achievements of civilised life, and which almost seems to anticipate the modern doctrines of evolutionary progress. But this idea does not dominate the thought of the poet. Behind it lies the sombre pessimism of the Lucretian world-view, in which the whole life of mankind is a momentary spark kindled and extinguished in the blind rush of material forces through infinite space and time. And even this qualified recognition of progress is exceptional; elsewhere it is almost completely absent.

What is the reason for this state of things? It was not due, as with the Indians, to any inherent pessimism in the minds of the Greeks, still less to any deficiency in their knowledge. On the contrary, it sprang from the very nature of the Greek scientific ideal. Greek thought was utterly unlike the science of the modern world, which seeks to unravel the secrets of nature one by one, by a laborious process of experimental research. It was impatient of partial solution. It aspired to comprehend the innermost nature of reality and to know the cosmic process as a whole.

The Greek universe, like the Greek statue, was a perfect and harmonious unity. From the time when Pythagoras first attempted to subject the changing appearances of the external world to mathematical laws and to view it as an intelligible harmony, this conception dominated all Greek thought. It found its completest expression in the Platonic cosmology with its picture of the world as "a sensible God, who is the image of the intelligible, greatest, best, most beautiful and most perfect—the one only-begotten universe."

Now this vision of the world *sub specie aeternitatis* made it impossible to attach any ultimate importance to the changes of the temporal process. For though the earth was not itself eternal, it was modelled on an eternal pattern, and time itself "imitates eternity, and moves in a circle measured by number." For since the perfect motion of the heavenly spheres is always circular, the process of temporal change must be circular also. It is not only plants and animals that go through a cycle of growth and decay— all created things have their appointed numbers and revolutions, and the cycle of the world and of time itself is fulfilled in the perfect year, when the heavens have performed a full revolution and the planets find themselves in the same relation to one another that they were at the beginning. Then the cosmic process begins anew and all things recur in their former order.

But the philosopher has no need to concern himself with the course of terrestrial change. It is his business to fix his attention on the intelligible forms from which the impermanent world of sense derives its existence, and to raise himself by scientific knowledge to the contemplation of the "colourless, shapeless, intangible Reality" which abides for ever in unchanging perfection. This is the Platonic world-view, and that of Aristotle is essentially similar, in spite of the differences in his physical explanation of the universe. To him also the highest knowledge was to be found in the contemplation of the universe as a manifestation of perfect and unchanging Being. All progress is but a part of the process of generation and corruption, which is confined to the sublunary world—*"the hollow of the Moon"*[45]—and which depends on the local movements of the heavenly spheres.

All such change must necessarily be cyclic. "For if," he says, "the movement of heaven appears periodic and eternal, then it is necessary that the details of this movement and all the effects produced by it will also be periodic and eternal."[46] Nor is this to be understood solely of material changes, for Aristotle expressly states that even the opinions of the philosophers themselves will recur in an identical form, "not once nor twice nor a few times, but to infinity."

On such an assumption the idea of progress must, of course, lose its meaning, since every movement of advance is at the same time a movement of return. Even the succession of time becomes a purely relative conception, as Aristotle himself very clearly shows. 'If it is true that the Universe has a beginning, a middle, and an end, and that that which has grown old and reached its end has thereby returned anew to its beginning, and if the earlier things are those that are nearest to the beginning, what is there to prevent our being anterior to the men who lived in the time of the

---

[45] *Meteora*, I, xiv. I owe these and the following quotations to P. Duhem, *Le Systeme du Monde*, vols. i and ii, in which the theories of Greek science regarding the Great Year are described in detail.

[46] *Met.*, I, iii.

Trojan War? Alcmæon has well said that men are mortal because they cannot join their end to their beginning. If the course of events is a circle, as the circle has neither beginning nor end, we cannot be anterior to the men of Troy, and they cannot be anterior to us, since neither of us are nearer to the beginning.'[47]

Not only is this point of view irreconcilable with a belief in progress, it seems to lead inevitably to the pessimistic fatalism of *Ecclesiastes*:

'That which hath been is that which shall be; and that which hath been done is that which shall be done: and there is no new thing under the sun. Is there a thing whereof men say, See, this is new? It hath been already, in the ages which were before us.'

And the same spirit dominates the thought of the Roman Stoics, and inspires the fatalistic quietism of Marcus Aurelius. 'The rational soul,' he says, 'traverses the whole universe and the surrounding void, and surveys its form and it extends itself into the infinity of time, and embraces and comprehends the periodical renovation of all things, and it comprehends that those who come after us will see nothing new, nor have those before us seen anything more, but in a manner he who is forty years old, if he has any understanding at all, has seen, by virtue of the uniformity that prevails, all things that have been and all that will be.'[48]

It is true that Aristotle tried to leave some room for contingency and free will, and denied the necessity

---

[47] *Problemata*, XVII, 3.

[48] M. Aurel. *Anton.,* XI, 1, Long's translation. Cf. Seneca, *Ep. ad Lucilium*, 24; *De Tranquillitate*, 1 and 2.

of the numerical identity of mankind in the different cycles. But other thinkers were more thoroughgoing in their application of the theory. 'According to the Pythagoreans,' says Eudemus, 'I shall be telling you the same story once more, holding the same staff in my hand, and you will be seated as you are at present, and all things will happen as before.' And Stoics, like Zeno and Chrysippus, were equally uncompromising. When the cycle of the Great Year has completed its revolution, Dion will be here again, the same man in the same body, only excepting, says Chrysippus, such details as the wart upon his face!

Indeed, the philosophers of the Hellenistic age went a step further, and taught that it was possible to foretell the next stage of the fated cycle from the study of the movements of the stars. We are so accustomed to think of astrology as a popular superstition that we are apt to forget how closely it was bound up with ancient science and philosophy. The astrological fatalism of Manilius is nearer in spirit to modern scientific determinism than to popular superstition, and the Aristotelian theory that the movement of the heavens is the efficient cause of earthly change seemed to provide a scientific basis for the most ambitious claims of the astrologers. Even the Neoplatonists, who were far less determinist than the other schools and preserved a high ideal of moral freedom and responsibility, did not deny the pre-established harmony between the events of the world below and the order of the heavens, though Plotinus conceived the stars not as causes, but as signs and ministers of the Eternal Mind.[49]

---

[49] Cf. his long discussion of the subject in Enn., II, iii, 7.

It is difficult to exaggerate the importance of these ideas in the history of ancient thought. They were not confined to a single age or to a single school. From the age of Pythagoras and Heracleitus down to the last days of the School of Athens under the Christian Emperors, the doctrine of the Great Year and the recurrent cycle of cosmic change dominated the Greek mind. Nor was it limited to Hellas. It was the common possession of all the great civilisations of the ancient world, and it is probable that the whole system springs from a common origin in Mesopotamia, where astronomy and astrology reached a high pitch of development during the Neo-Babylonian period.

In addition to Babylonia, we find it in Syria and Persia and India, and even as far east as China, where it has remained current down to the present day. Indeed, the Chinese astrologers surpass the Greeks in the exactitude with which they have calculated every phase of the cosmic cycle.[50]

There remained, however, one people whose attitude to the world was fundamentally different. To the Jews, history possessed a unique and absolute value, such as no other people of antiquity had conceived. The Eternal Law, which the Greeks saw manifested in the movement of the heavenly spheres, was embodied for the Jews in the vicissitudes of human history. While the philosophers of India and Greece were meditating on the illusoriness or the eternity of the cosmic process, the Prophets of Israel were affirming

---

[50] The Chinese Great Year consists of twelve months or " Confluences,'" each of which is as long as the Great Year, which the Greeks ascribed to Heracleitas, i.e., 10,800 years. We have now reached the year 68,943 of the whole cycle, and in the following Great Month the period of the decline of Heaven and Earth will begin.

the moral government of the universe and the passing events of their age as the manifestation of a divine purpose.

From the beginning the eyes of Jahweh had been fixed on this little Palestinian people, which was his chosen vehicle, and the great world empires, whose clash destroyed the independence and the very national existence of Israel, were but the instruments of this transcendent purpose. Thus all history was moving towards a great consummation: the revelation of the power and the glory of Jahweh through his servant Israel, and the eternal reign of justice in the Messianic Kingdom of God.

Here then we have a conception of history which is clearly progressive, but it is a progress which fulfils itself only through the interposition of supernatural forces, not through the natural course of human development. It is, in fact, essentially eschatological.

The eschatological idea was not, of course, exclusively Jewish. It had already appeared in early Zoroastrianism. But while in Persia it became subordinated to the cyclic theory, among the Jews it was inseparably connected with the realities of national history.

It is true that the idea of the world-cycle had become so universal that the Jews could not altogether escape its influence, and we find in the later Jewish apocalyptic literature frequent references to the *zōn* or world-age. But the *zōn* in Jewish apocalyptic is not a cycle: it is a period or dispensation of a single, unique process.

And with the appearance of Christianity, the Jewish world-view and the Jewish eschatology acquired a new and wider development. To the Christian, and above all to St Paul, the key to world history was found in the Incarnation, which was viewed not merely as the realisation of the Messianic hope of the Jewish people, but as the restoration of mankind and of the whole material creation. Christ is the head of this restored humanity, the firstborn of the new creation, and the life of the Church consists in the gradual incorporation of mankind into this higher unity.

Hence, in spite of the Christian opposition between "this world" and "the world to come," there could be no tampering with the reality and uniqueness of the historical process. The irreconcilability of Christianity with the dominant theory of cosmic cycles is obvious, and was stated uncompromisingly by the early Fathers. If we accept that theory, says Origen, "then Adam and Eve will do in a second world exactly as they have done in this; the same deluge will be repeated; the same Moses will bring the same people out of Egypt, Judas will a second time betray his Lord, and again Paul will keep the garments of those who will stone Stephen."[51]

And it was on this very ground that the Church had to fight its earliest battles, for Gnosticism was essentially an attempt to combine the belief in spiritual redemption with the theory of world-eons and of the illusory nature of earthly change, and consequently the whole anti-Gnostic apologia of St Irenaeus is directed to the defence of the value and reality of the historical development.

"Since men are real, theirs must be a real establishment. They do not vanish into non-existence, but progress among existent things." "There is one Son who performs the Father's will, and one human race in which the mysteries of God are realised" (Iren. *adv.*

---

[51] *Peri Archon*, lib. II, ch. iii, 4-5. Cf. St Aug., *De Civ. Dei*, XII, 13.

Her., V, 36, 1). "God arranged everything from the first with a view to the perfection of man, in order to edify him and reveal His own dispensations, so that goodness may be made manifest, justice made perfect, and the Church may be fashioned after the image of His Son. Thus man may eventually reach maturity, and being ripened by such privileges, may see and comprehend God" (IV, 37, 7).[52]

This strong emphasis on what Bousset calls the *Evolutionsgedanke* in Irenaeus was carried by Tertullian beyond the bounds of orthodoxy, since it led him to deny the final character of the Christian revelation. "There is growth," he says, "in everything. We see it in nature with the quickening of the seed, the growth of the plant, and the ripening of the fruit, and so also it is in the spiritual world, for it is the same God that works in both. The development of humanity begins with the fear of God; the Jewish dispensation is the age of childhood, with the Gospel it bursts forth into youth, and finally maturity comes with the Age of the Spirit, who is henceforth the sole master of humanity" (*De Virginibus*, I).

This evolutionary millenarianism with its scheme of the three Ages of Humanity was destined to have a long career in the history of human thought, and it even contributed directly, as we shall see, to the formation of the modern idea of Progress. But the conception of Progress was equally present in orthodox thought and found its fullest expression in the writings of St Augustine. His *City of God* is the first attempt to write a Christian philosophy of history, and its influence has dominated the thought of Western Christendom ever since.

---

[52] Tr. F. M. Hitchcock.

He views the whole course of history as the result of the development and conflict of two societies—the City of God, animated by divine charity, and the city of This World, based upon materialism and self-love—both growing together until the final consummation, in which the City of God will be established for ever. Thus out of the evil and disorder of human history an ultimate harmony is being evolved, for "God is the unchangeable governor, as he is the unchangeable Creator of all mutable things, ordering all events in His Providence, until the beauty of the completed course of time, the component parts of which are the dispensations adapted to each successive age, shall be finished, like the perfect melody of a great musician" (*Epistle to Marcellinus*, 138).

But this ultimate optimism and belief in spiritual progress is combined with a definitely pessimistic attitude towards the present world. To some extent this is due to the circumstances of the age to the decline of the Roman Empire and the belief in the approaching end of the world. But it has a deeper cause in that "otherworldliness" which is an essential part of the Christian attitude to life. Men have here no continuing city. They are strangers and pilgrims on the earth. Their true home is in heaven. The progress of material civilisation is not an absolute end. Indeed, in so far as it distracts men's minds from their true goal, it may be positively harmful.

Thus the idea of Progress was absent from the Christian Middle Ages, no less than from pagan antiquity. It only began to make its appearance with the growing secularisation of European culture that took place after the Renaissance. Nevertheless, it was not a new original creation, like modern science or Renaissance art. It arose spontaneously from the survival of the Christian ethical and teleological view of human development in a secularised environment: it was the natural faith of a society which had inherited the tradition of Christian thought, but had lost its belief in the Christian revelation.

For a civilisation cannot strip itself of its past in the same way that a philosopher discards a theory. The religion that has governed the life of a people for a thousand years enters into its very being, and moulds all its thought and feeling. When the philosophers of the eighteenth century attempted to substitute their new rationalist doctrines for the ancient faith of Christendom, they were in reality simply abstracting from it those elements which had entered so deeply into their own thought that they no longer recognised their origin. Eighteenth-century Deism was but the ghost or shadow of Christianity, a mental abstraction from the reality of a historical religion, which possesses no independent life of its own. It retained certain fundamental Christian conceptions—the belief in a beneficent Creator, the idea of an overruling Providence which ordered all things for the best, and the chief precepts of the Christian moral law, but all these were desupernaturalised and fitted into the utilitarian rational scheme of contemporary philosophy. Thus the moral law was divested of all ascetic and otherworldly elements and assimilated to practical philanthropy, and the order of Providence was transformed into a mechanistic natural law. Above all this was the case with the idea of Progress, for while the new philosophy had no place for the supernaturalism of the Christian eschatology, it could not divest itself of the Christian teleological conception of life. Thus the belief in the moral perfectibility and the indefinite progress of the human race took the place of the Christian faith in the life of the world to come as the final goal of human effort. This idea lies at the root of the whole philosophic movement, and it was fully formulated long before the days of the Encyclopédist propaganda. And it is quite in accordance with what I have said regarding the origins of this circle of ideas, that its author should have been a priest—the first of that long line of sceptical and reforming clerics, such as Mably, Condillac, Morelly, Raynal, and Sieyés, who were so characteristic of the Age of Enlightenment.

The Abbé de St Pierre was a prophet who received little honour in his own country. He had the reputation of a crank and a bore. It was for his statue that Voltaire wrote the lines:

ce n'est là qu'un portrait.
L'original dirait quelque sottise.

Yet his fertile brain originated most of the projects that were to be realised or attempted by the liberals of the next two centuries—international arbitration and the abolition of war, free education and the reform of female education, the establishment of a poor rate and the abolition of pauperism, not to mention other inventions peculiar to himself such as the social utilisation of sermons. But underlying all this was his fundamental doctrine of the "perpetual and unlimited augmentation of the universal human reason," which will inevitably produce the golden age and the establishment of paradise on earth. Nor would this happy consummation be long delayed. All that was necessary was the conversion of the powers that be to the Abbé's principles, for St Pierre shared the beliefs of his age as to the unlimited possibilities of governmental action.

And this doctrine became the ruling conception of the new age, for while the God of the Deists was but a pale abstraction, a mere *deus ex machina*, the belief in Progress was an ideal capable of stirring men's emotions and arousing a genuine religious enthusiasm. Nor was it limited to the followers of the French philosophic rationalism. It played an equally important part in the formation of German idealism and English utilitarian Liberalism. In England, its derivation from theological presuppositions is particularly clear. Its chief exponents, Price and Priestley, were Nonconformist ministers, and the earlier theorists of progress in Great Britain, Turnbull and, above all, David Hartley, rested their whole argument on a theological basis. The turbid flood of English Puritanism had spread in the eighteenth century into the wide and shallow waters of Liberal Protestantism, and the visionary millenarian ideas of the earlier period had been transformed into a rational enthusiasm for moral and material progress. Even the economic doctrines of Adam Smith rest on a foundation of religious optimism, which remained a characteristic feature of later British Liberalism.

At first sight the contemporary movement in France is the diametrical opposite of this, since it was marked by a bitter hostility to Christianity. But we must not be misled by the anti-religious diatribes of the French philosophers. Real scepticism is usually tolerant, and the intolerance and iconoclasm of the eighteenth-century philosophers, like that of the sixteenth-century Reformers, was the fanaticism of the sectaries of a new gospel. The French Enlightenment was, in fact, the last of the great European heresies, and its appeal to Reason was in itself an act of faith which admitted of no criticism. Even materialists like

Helvétius and Holbach shared the Deist belief in the transcendence of Reason and the inevitability of intellectual and moral progress, though there was nothing in their premises to warrant such assumptions.

Moreover, the movement of philosophic rationalism was only one side of the French eighteenth-century development. No less important was the social idealism of Rousseau, which was far more pronouncedly religious in spirit. Rousseau was at once a revolutionary and a reactionary of the type of Tolstoy. He turned away from modern civilisation and the creed of scientific progress towards the simplicity of an idealised state of nature, and though he believed no less intensely than Diderot or Condorcet in the perfectibility of man and society, he looked for its realisation, not to Reason and external organisation, but to the inner light of conscience and to obedience to the eternal laws of nature that are written in the human heart.

At first sight, it would seem that this pessimism and "otherworldliness" leaves little room for any belief in Progress, but Rousseau's appeal to the inherent rights of man and his belief in the possibility of an abrupt reconstitution of absolute principles aroused the enthusiasm of the men of his age and became the inspiration of the whole European revolutionary movement. If the earlier philosophic doctrine of Progress, with its dogmatic appeal to the authority of Reason and its reliance on an enlightened despotism, represents the secularisation of the orthodox Christian view of life, the revolutionary idealism of Rousseau has an even closer affinity with the apocalyptic hopes of the earlier millenniarists and Anabaptists. Indeed, it is often difficult to distinguish the descriptions of the social millennium of the revolutionaries from those of the religious apocalyptic. "In that blessed day," writes Godwin, the leading English representative of revolutionary idealism, "there will be no war, no crimes, no administration of justice, as it is called, and no government. Besides this, there will be neither disease, anguish, melancholy, nor resentment. Every man will seek with ineffable ardour the good of all. Mind will be active and eager, and yet never disappointed."[53]

So, too, Godwin's son-in-law and disciple, Shelley, in spite of his worship of Hellenic antiquity, unconsciously derived his ideals from the religious tradition which he so bitterly attacked. What could be more Christian than the whole idea of *Prometheus Unbound*, the salvation of humanity by the suffering and love of an innocent victim? And in the same way, too, Shelley's ideal of liberty is utterly foreign to the tradition of Hellenism. It is nothing less than "the glorious liberty of the children of God," for which the whole creation groans, and the effects of which overflow from humanity to the external world, and transform the whole order of nature.

This millenniarist conception of Progress is specially characteristic of the early Socialists. It reaches its climax in Fourier, whose speculations surpass in extravagance the wildest dreams of Cerinthus and his followers. For according to Fourier all the present evils of the material world are bound up with our defective social arrangements. Nature is bad because man is bad. As soon as the new social order of the Fourierist gospel is introduced the earth will be transformed. The waters of the ocean will change to lemonade, and the useless and ugly marine monsters,

---

[53] W. Godwin, *Inquiry Concerning Political Justice*, II, 528

which are the images of our own passions, will be replaced by useful and agreeable creatures. Human life will be extended to three or four centuries, and there will be 37,000,000 poets equal to Homer, and 37,000,000 philosophers like Aristotle.

In comparison with Fourier, Robert Owen and the St Simonians appear mere cautious rationalists, but nevertheless millenniarist ideals colour all their thoughts and were transmitted by them to the later political Socialism. The driving force of the Socialist movement, in fact, has always been its belief in a social apocalypse.

Karl Marx shared this belief with the Utopian Socialists, whom he criticised. He rationalised it by his scientific materialism, but he did not remove it. The main difference between the two conceptions lies in the fact that Marx, who inherited the Jewish religious attitude, looked for its realisation to the inevitable working of eternal laws outside human control, whereas St Simon and Fourier, who were Christians at least by historical tradition, based their hopes on the conversion of the individual will and the moral *perfectment* of humanity.

But while the origin of Socialism is primarily due to the economic interpretation of the revolutionary idealism of Rousseau, it also owed much to the influence of German thought. Now in Germany the theory of Progress had developed on different lines to those that it followed in France, its original home. The German philosophers did not share the open hostility to Christianity that marked the French Enlightenment; indeed, some of them were deeply influenced by the mystical ideas of German Pietism. Moreover, they had a much wider and deeper appreciation of history than their French predecessors. Instead of emphasising the contradiction between the Age of Reason and the Age of Faith, they brought Christianity and historical religion into their scheme of progress. Thus Lessing in his famous booklet *On the Education of the Human Race* bases his philosophy of history on a progressive religious revelation, which he assimilates to the doctrine of Tertullian and Joachim of Flora concerning the three world ages of the Christian dispensation.

The Third Age of the Reign of the Spirit and the Eternal Gospel was conceived by Lessing as the Age of Reason and of the self-realisation of humanity, but it was the fulfilment, not the contradiction, of the Christian revelation.

The influence of Lessing's theory was extraordinarily deep and far-reaching. It lies at the root of the development of Liberal or Modernist Protestantism in Germany, it affected the St Simonian Socialists in France,[54] and even Comte's famous Law of the Three Stages was probably influenced by it. Above all, it was adopted with enthusiasm by all the great German idealist philosophers, each of whom interpreted it according to the requirements of his own system. Schelling conceives the Third Age in the spirit of the Abbot Joachim himself, as the restoration of all things in Christ. "We know not when that age will be," he says, "but when it will be, God will be." To Hegel, on the other hand, political history is the progressive revelation of God, and it is in the modern Prussian State that the Eternal Spirit attains its final realisation.

---

[54] *The Education of the Human Race* was translated by E. Rodriguez, the St Simonian, when Comte was still a member of the group.

But Hegel already stands at the parting of the ways. On the one hand, he is in contact with the mysticism of Schelling; on the other, with the historical materialism of Marx. In the earlier idealist movement the dependence on the Christian tradition is open and admitted, and consequently throughout the earlier part of the nineteenth century, alike in Germany and France, with St Simon and Comte, and Buchez and Leroux, as well as with Schelling and Schlegel, there is a tendency to emphasise the importance of religion, and to base the doctrine of Progress on a religious foundation. But from the middle of the century the intellectual atmosphere of Europe changes. There is a sharp reaction against the romantic idealism of the previous period, and at the same time a renewal of the eighteenth-century criticism of religion. This owed something to political disillusionment, and the failure of the revolutionary programme on the Continent, but it was due, above all, to the advance of science, and a more thorough-going application of the new scientific principles to the facts of human development.

The eighteenth-century philosophers, even when they were materialists, consciously placed man in a category above and apart from the rest of nature, and hypostatised human reason into a principle of world development. But the new evolutionary theory of the Origin of Species put man back into Nature, and ascribed his development to the mechanical operation of the same blind forces which ruled the material world. The eighteenth-century doctrine of Progress was, as we have seen, essentially Deist in origin, and depended on the belief in an overruling Providence. The new scientific outlook, on the other hand, eliminated all teleological conceptions. Science had no need of such a hypothesis, as Laplace said to Napoleon. The earlier theory of Evolution as formulated by Lamarck, who was a disciple of Condorcet, and founded on theological presuppositions, was dominated by the optimist doctrine of Progress. Darwinism, however, arose under the influence of the objective and pessimistic views of Malthus. The theory of Natural Selection and the survival of the fittest was the Malthusian doctrine of the pressure of population upon food supply elevated to a cosmic law. It was a law of Progress, but a non-ethical progress in which suffering and death played a larger part than foresight or co-operation. In Darwin's words, "From the war of nature, from famine and death, the most exalted object that we are capable of conceiving, namely, the production of the higher animals, directly follows."

This view of evolution has been considerably modified by the post-Darwinian biologists, but in his own age it was the central doctrine of the new science. It was accepted by Darwin himself in a spirit of religious faith — the "O Altitudo" of the mystic — but to his rationalist followers it was profoundly disquieting, since it suggested an opposition not between Religion and Science, but between the law of human Progress and the law of natural development. Man with his high ethical ideals was the product and plaything of a "Nature red in tooth and claw." "Social Progress," says Huxley, "means the checking of the cosmic process at every step, and the substitution for it of another, which may be called ethical progress." But if this is so, how can man's puny efforts avail against the eternal course of nature? We are led inevitably to the defiant pessimism which Mr Bertrand Russell has expressed so eloquently in one of his essays: "Brief and powerless is man's life; on him and all his race the slow sure doom falls, pitiless and dark. Blind to good and evil, reckless of destruction, omnipotent matter rolls on its relentless way; for man, condemned to-day to lose his dearest, to-morrow himself to pass through the gates of darkness, it remains only to cherish ere yet the blow falls the lofty thoughts that ennoble his little day; disclaiming the coward terrors of the slave of Fate, to worship at the shrine that his own hands have built; undismayed by the empire of chance, to preserve a mind free from the wanton tyranny that rules his outward life; proudly defiant of the irresistible forces that tolerate for a moment his knowledge and his condemnation, to sustain alone, a weary but unyielding Atlas, the world that his own ideals have fashioned despite the trampling march of unconscious power."[55]

This is, after all, but the last effort of an expiring romanticism. If man has nothing else left, let him at least keep his heroic attitude. *Vive le panache!* But it is a poor substitute for the dogmatic certitude of the old belief in Progress, for Condorcet's vision of "mankind marching with a firm tread on the road of truth, virtue and happiness," with no limit to its hopes and no fear of disillusionment. So long as science was the servant of the optimistic Deist creed, it was itself optimistic; but as soon as science came into its kingdom, its optimism began to disappear. Nor was this solely due to the influence of the Darwinian version of the Evolutionary Theory; it lies in the very nature of the materialistic world-view. When once we abandon the theological doctrine of Creation, which is common both to orthodox Christianity and to the

---

[55] B. Russell, "A Free Man's Worship" in *Mysticism and Logic*, p. 56.

philosophic Deism which is derived from it, we are left with an eternal cosmic process, which does not admit of ultimate and absolute progress. The development of our planet is but a momentary result of material laws, which, working in infinite time and space, must repeat themselves endlessly, and so we are brought back to the cyclic theory of the Return of All Things, and once more we shall say with Lucretius:

eadem sunt omnia semper.

It is true that this belief no longer has the same scientific justification that it possessed for the Hellenic cosmologists. Indeed, it is not easy to reconcile their fundamental doctrine of the eternity of the universe with the principles of the modern science of thermodynamics, as established by Carnot and interpreted by Lord Kelvin. The law of the Degradation of Energy suggests, as Kelvin pointed out, that the universe is slowly but inevitably travelling towards eternal death, since the energy that has once been dissipated or rendered inactive can never be reconstituted. The clock of nature is gradually running down, and so far as our knowledge goes, there is no natural process by which it can ever be wound up again. Thus the cosmic process is apparently not circular, as the Greeks believed, but moves in a single irreversible direction. It has a beginning, and must ultimately have an end, though in the intervening period there is room for an uncounted number of worlds and cycles. Change is not mere illusion; it is the ultimate reality of the physical universe.

Nevertheless, the idea of an absolute beginning or end is so repugnant to anyone who does not accept a theistic or non-mechanical world view, that it has never been fully assimilated by the modern scientific mind. From Herbert Spencer and Haeckel to Arrhenius and Becquerel there has been a whole series of attempts to provide new scientific justification for the mechanistic theory of an eternal recurrence; and though none of these has yet been successful, there is no reason to think that the cyclical theory has been finally abandoned.

However, the discussion of these problems has been confined to the scientific world, and has hitherto had no influence worth recording on the development of the doctrine of Progress.

Indeed, during the later nineteenth century the belief in progress became more widespread than ever before. But it was ceasing to be a philosophic doctrine, and had become an idol of the market-place. It now rested on the self-confidence of a prosperous society, which justified its high hopes for the future by the growth in wealth and population that had been actually realised. Our civilisation was the only civilisation, and its endurance and progress were unquestioned.

But this facile optimism has received a rude shock since the European War. The permanence of the European industrial scientific order is no longer unchallenged. We have witnessed the passing of the economic hegemony from Europe to America, the Russian revolution, and the reaction of the Oriental civilisations against the supremacy of the West. Above all, we have seen in Europe itself the decay of the liberal tradition which was not merely responsible for the English Victorian compromise, but which has dominated the main current of European culture since the eighteenth century. Liberalism, with its optimistic faith in Progress and Enlightenment, is giving place either to Socialism or to a national dictatorship resting upon force. And even Socialism itself is losing its visionary hopes. The Communist Utopia has gone the way of the Utopia of the Jacobins, and the Socialism of the near future will be a realist Socialism, which will concern itself with the practical task of keeping the population clothed and fed, rather than with schemes for the perfecting of humanity.

In so far, therefore, as the creed of Progress rested on a belief in the growing material prosperity and security of our civilisations, its foundations are already shaken, and we are growing accustomed to the idea that our civilisation is but one civilisation among many, with no greater claim to permanence than those of past ages. On the Continent the application of the cyclic theory to the phenomena of cultural change has attained almost as great a popularity as the old theory of indefinite progress.

And as we have seen, the outlook of modern science affords no surer foundation for the theory.

The day of the Deist and liberal compromise is over, and we have come to the parting of the ways. Either the belief in Progress will be finally abandoned in favour of the old philosophy of eternal changeless change, or the European culture must return consciously to the Christian tradition from which it has sprung. The modern world has not lost the need for religion. The value and, indeed, the necessity of a religious interpretation of life is felt more strongly than ever, and science no longer attempts, as in the previous period, to deny its legitimacy. But the religious impulse must express itself consciously through religious channels, and not seek a furtive illegitimate expression in scientific or political theories to the detriment alike of religion and of science. The Judeo-Christian world-view, and that alone, justifies a reasonable faith in human progress and in the unique value of human experience, but it must be recognised that this faith rests on religious foundations, and that it cannot be severed from historical religion and used as a substitute for it, as it has been during the last two centuries.

Christopher Dawson, 1927

7

THE CRISIS OF THE WEST

OF ALL the changes that the twentieth century has brought, none goes deeper than the loss of that unquestioning faith in the future and in the absolute value of our civilisation, which was the dominant note of the nineteenth century.

The Great War, and still more the period of disillusionment and economic strain that followed it, has caused men to realise what a fragile thing civilisation is, and how insecure are the foundations on which the elaborate edifice of modern society rests.

Moreover, the European crisis and the weakening of social stability have given an opportunity to all the forces that were hostile to the nineteenth-century order. The Russian Revolution supplied a rallying-point and a model of action for all the discontented elements in Western society, and in — country a vigorous propaganda is being carried on in favour of the Communist programme of class war and social revolution. At the same time the peoples of the East are in revolt against Western imperialism, and against the economic and social dependence of Asia on European civilisation.

But perhaps the most serious symptom of all is the spirit of pessimism and disillusionment which prevails so widely among the leaders of opinion in Europe itself. In the nineteenth century both the reformers and the conservatives were fundamentally optimistic, with an immense belief in the superiority of modern civilisation and a sturdy confidence in the future. Today we find Socialists like Mr Bertrand Russell who believe that the civilisation of modern Europe has lost all moral justification and has become a menace to the human race, while many of the ablest conservative thinkers in this country, and still more on the Continent, maintain that it is all up with England and with Europe, and that our civilisation has entered on a phase of inevitable decline, like that which brought about the fall of Rome and so many other flourishing cultures of ancient times. Thus, in the prevalent mood of pessimism and national self-depreciation, there is a general tendency to deny or underrate the value of the nineteenth-century achievement.

The revolutionary takes it for granted as the bad old order of things against which he rebels; the reactionary is prepared to wipe it off the slate as a failure. Neither of them understands that the nineteenth century was one of the great creative epochs in the history of the human race — that it was not an age like other ages, but a rare peak of achievement, after the attainment of which the life of humanity can never be the same as it was before. It entails a radical modification of men's relation to their environment, for it marks the definite conquest of nature by man, the taming of the tyranny of circumstance, and the harnessing of the forces of brute matter by the power of human intelligence. This change was indeed implicit in the great scientific discoveries of the seventeenth century, and its possibility was already envisaged by thinkers like Bacon and Descartes, and even Campanella and Leonardo da Vinci. For it was the abstract thinkers, and not the men of action, who were the creators of the new civilisation.

As Henri Poincaré has well said, "The conquests of industry, which have enriched so many practical men, would never have seen the day if these practical men had been the only ones to exist, and if they had not been preceded by disinterested madmen, who died poor, who never thought of the useful, but who nevertheless were guided by something more than their own caprices."[56]

The greatness of the nineteenth century consists in the fact that it was an age both of great thinkers and of great men of action — of "disinterested madmen" like Cauchy and Gauss, Faraday and Clerk Maxwell, as well as of the captains of industry, the financiers and the engineers, who planned the railways, and sank the shafts, and laid the cables which have transformed the face of the earth. And all these individual activities are but the manifestation of the great co-operative effort by which Western society summoned up its forces for the conquest of the world.

---

[56] *Science et Méthode*, p. 9.

We have grown so accustomed to look at the dark side of the Industrial Revolution, the ruthlessness of the factory system, and the selfishness of the capitalists and the profiteers that we are apt to forget the elements of self-sacrifice and asceticism that characterised the beginnings of Industrialism. Historians such as Troeltsch and Max Weber have shown that the origins of the modern industrial movement have a very close connection with the moral and social ideals of Puritanism. The Protestant asceticism of the seventeenth and eighteenth centuries did not lead men to fly from the world and give up all their goods to the poor as in the Middle Ages. On the contrary, it inculcated the duty of an unremitting industry and thrift, while at the same time rigorously discountenancing any kind of self-indulgence or extravagance in the expenditure of what had been gained. This was the ideal of the classes that contributed most to the economic revolution, and it favoured the rise of that type of man who was so characteristic of English and American middle-class society a century ago—the hard-headed, hard-working conscientious man of business who spared himself no more than his employees and looked on his work as a sort of religious vocation.

Just as the ideal of disinterested scientific knowledge made possible the technical achievements of the nineteenth-century culture, the narrow and intense Puritan religious ideal gave the latter its moral driving power. Without this intense conviction of a providential mission the Western peoples—above all the "Anglo-Saxons"—could never have made so deep an impression on the rest of the world. Religion went hand in hand with trade to the conquest of the earth. It inspired soldiers and administrators like Gordon and Lawrence no less than missionaries and explorers like Livingstone and George Grenfell, and the flag followed the missionary into the remotest regions of Africa and the Pacific. Thus in the course of the nineteenth century this combination of economic expansion, missionary propaganda, and military conquest has led Europe step by step to a position of world hegemony.

The great Oriental civilisations which have existed for ages as closed worlds have been drawn into the net of the new industrial scientific culture of the West. By the twentieth century, regions in Africa the very existence of which were unknown a century earlier were producing wealth for the European market, and were in closer economic relations with England than England herself had been with the Continent in the eighteenth century, while in America and Australia great modern cities with hundreds of thousands of inhabitants had sprung up on the hunting-grounds of savage tribes, whose manner of life had little changed since palæolithic times.

Nor is this expansion of European culture confined to colonisation and economic penetration. There is also a general process of assimilation owing to which the non-European peoples are adopting Western manners and dress, Western arms and military organisation, Western education and political institutions. Republics and parliaments on the

Western model have replaced sacred monarchies that had ruled from immemorial antiquity. Everywhere the old independent cultural ideals and the old self-sufficient agrarian economy have broken down, and the world has become a single community with an international economic life and common political and educational standards.

The whole process bears a remarkable resemblance to the unification of the ancient world by Rome in the first and second centuries B.C., though it is on a vaster scale and involves far wider issues. It is true that the Roman Imperial movement was essentially military and the economic factor was secondary, whereas the modern world organisation is primarily economic and the military aspect of it has been subordinate. Nevertheless, the builders of the Roman roads were fulfilling the same function as the constructors of the modern railways; and the Roman financiers and societies of publicans took the same part in the development of the Empire as the European capitalists and bond-holders in modern times. Cicero's famous speech in support of military intervention in Asia Minor might almost have been made by an English politician at the time of the South African War, except for its outspoken naïveté. "Unless the enemy is quickly suppressed," he says, "not only will the publicans themselves, who are the prop and support of all the other orders of society, use their wealth, but so will all the private citizens who have invested their money in Asia, and this in turn will produce a series of failures on the Roman Forum. For Roman credit and the state of the money market are inextricably bound up with the capital invested in Asia. So now," he concludes, "see if you can hesitate to throw all your energies into a war in which you are defending at once national glory, public revenues, and private investments."[57]

The Roman, no less than the Victorian Englishman, was fully convinced of his inborn superiority to the clever and immoral Greeks and the superstitious and feckless Orientals. He also inherited a strict moral code, and a high ideal of duty and labouriousness from the religion of his peasant ancestors. A type like the elder Cato, with his forbidding appearance — "all teeth and red hair," as a contemporary said — his moral censoriousness, his personal probity, and his devotion to money-making, is utterly alien to the modern Italian character, but finds plenty of parallels in the England of the Industrial Revolution. But it was the Nemesis of this society that it destroyed the foundations on which its own strength rested. The old Roman virtues withered away when the peasant republic had become a capitalist oligarchy, based on a mercenary army and a horde of tax-gatherers. The successors of the Catonian tradition — model republicans like Brutus — were millionaires, who exploited the provinces and lent great sums of money to subject communities at an interest of 48 per cent. The smallholdings of the citizen farmers were absorbed by the vast estates of the new nobility, worked by cheap slave labour imported from abroad, while their former owners

---

[57] *Pro Lege Manilia*, VII.

drifted away to become mercenaries or to join the ranks of the urban proletariat, who lived by State doles, and were ready material for the revolutionary agitators. Meanwhile, would-be reformers attempted to mend matters by applying the remedies of Greek social democracy — the confiscation of the great estates and the proscription of the capitalist class. Thus, in the first century B.C., Roman society was faced by a revolutionary crisis, complicated by the rebellion of the subject nationalities and the horrors of a civil war. It seemed as though society would tear itself to pieces, and that the complete collapse of ancient civilisation was at hand.

Now in the modern world also economic progress and the success of material organisation have been accompanied by a process of social disorganisation, which produces grave discontent and the danger of a revolutionary crisis.

The capitalist organisation of industry has led, no less than military conquest, to the exploitation of subject classes and nationalities. It is true that modern industrialism at its worst has never led to the horrors of the Roman slave system, but the existence of the modern ideals of humanity and liberty has caused the evils of the modern system to be far more strongly felt. And it must be admitted that the industrial movement, while raising the general standard of life, has caused a retrogression in the position of the ordinary worker. Politically he gained full rights of citizenship such as he never possessed at any other period of the world's history; economically he lost the control that the craftsman possessed under the old system of hand industry over the conditions of his work, and became a mere cog in the vast machinery of modern industrialism.

Consequently, it was inevitable that the earlier revolutionary propaganda on behalf of the Rights of Man should ultimately take an economic form.

Socialism was, in fact, the heir of the earlier revolutionary Liberalism. In spite of the scientific interpretation that it received at the hands of Karl Marx and his disciples, it was like the doctrine of Rousseau—no cold rational theory, but a creed and a religion. It owed its popular appeal to the belief in a social apocalypse, the coming of a kingdom of justice, in which the poor and the oppressed should triumph, and the rich and the oppressor should be cast into outer darkness. All the great Socialists were equally Utopians. The only difference was that Marx believed that his Utopia would be won by the bomb and the rifle, while Godwin and Owen and St. Simon believed that it would come by a change of heart and a reign of universal benevolence. The Marxian interpretation of history and social evolution must be judged as an economic, or rather philosophic, theory; but, considered as a sociological phenomenon, the revolutionary socialism of modern Europe must be classed with the obscure movements of revolt that shook the ancient world in the first and second centuries B.C. It marks the failure of the great movement of material progress and organisation to satisfy the instincts of the human element, on whose labour the social edifice rests. It is not merely a dissatisfaction with material conditions; it is a movement of spiritual disaffection against the modern social order and a demand for a new life.

But it is not only the Socialists and the revolutionaries who threaten the modern European order. As in the case of the militarist capitalism of the later Roman Republic, the greatest danger to the industrialist capitalism of modern Europe comes from its own inherent instability.

The exploitation of the world by the new industrialised societies of Western Europe, like that of the Mediterranean lands by Rome in the first and second centuries B.C., has been too rapid to continue indefinitely.

The prosperity of the industrialised societies of the nineteenth century rested on a temporary monopoly of the new methods—on a limited output combined with a continually expanding world market.

But today these factors are reversed. The new methods are becoming common to the whole world, and the old monopoly enjoyed by the leading industrial Powers of Western Europe is rapidly disappearing. Every nation—even those of the Far East, like Japan—is organising itself to take its share in the world markets, while at the same time restricting those markets by a rigorous protective tariff.

Nowhere has the influence of these new conditions been felt more strongly than in England, the classical home of the old industry. At the present moment we see its effects, not only in the crisis of the coal industry, but in the disastrous state of all the so-called "heavy industries" subsisting by the foreign market, which has resulted in the work of a dustman being often better paid than that of a skilled engineer. Moreover, during the period of Free Trade and open markets the industrial population increased far beyond the limits of the national agricultural capacity, so that England is almost entirely dependent on an imported food supply, which must be financed by the industrial export, in the face of growing competition abroad and prohibitive duties.

Thus the vast and rapid development of the new economic order has produced a serious reaction, and Europe's position of world leadership seems threatened less than a century after its attainment. For if the organisation of the world by Europe was in the main due to her economic supremacy, the passing of that supremacy would seem to portend the breakdown of her international leadership. Already the East is reacting against the supremacy of the West and claiming an equality of position; and the internal power of resistance of European civilisation is weakened alike by national rivalry and disunion, and by the social discontent of international labour.

The ancient world passed through a similar crisis in the age of Mithridates and the Civil Wars. Then also the power of the West was threatened alike by the reaction of the Oriental world, and by its own disunity and the forces of social revolution. Had Rome failed the whole history of the world would have been different, but she succeeded in surmounting her difficulties at the cost of immense suffering; and, thanks to the achievements of the

Augustan age, the Roman work of material unification became the basis of a new order which has influenced the whole later development of civilisation.

In our own days the future of civilisation depends no less on the solution of the present crisis. If modern Europe breaks down, either through internal revolution or through loss of her world leadership, modern civilisation falls with her. For that civilisation was entirely a European creation, and there is no force outside Europe today capable of carrying on her work, whatever might be the case a century or two later.

Either the incipient world order that has been the work of the last century of Western progress will break down and disappear, or it must be completed by a further process of stabilisation and organisation which will make possible an age of true world civilisation under Western leadership. Now modern Europe is faced with three great problems.

First there is the international problem — the reconciliation of the claims of nationality with the unity and common interests of European culture.

Secondly, there is the Oriental problem — the reconciliation of the legitimate claims of the subject and dependent peoples of Asia and Africa with the leadership of Western culture.

And thirdly there is the economic problem — not only the reconciliation of the demand of labour for a higher standard of life with the capitalist control and organisation of industry, but also the whole problem of stabilising economic conditions and adjusting the relations of the industrial societies to the world markets and to the sources of supply. All these problems are especially vital to the future of this country, for the British Empire occupies a unique position between Europe and the East, as well as between Europe and the New World, and if it is no longer the leading industrial power of the world, it still retains economic supremacy as the centre of world finance and international trade.[58]

Moreover, it is in Great Britain that the problem of the relations of capital and labour is most acute, and it is generally recognised that the fate of the present economic order depends on its stability in this country.

It is, of course, far too early to foresee how these problems will find a solution, or whether they will find a solution at all. Socialism, of course, is one alternative, and in so far as the Socialists predict the growing control and organisation of economic life by the State, they are undoubtedly right. The great State has come to stay, and we can never return to the old individualism and laissez-faire of the Early Victorian age. But State organisation in itself is no solution; it merely heightens the bitterness of national economic rivalry. And here the Socialist panacea of world revolution is far more likely to hasten the collapse of Europe than to avert it. The capitalist organisation of industry and trade has played the same part in the unification of the modern world that the military

---

[58] i.e. as of 1927 when this was written.

organisation of Rome played in the ancient world, and Rome was saved not by revolutionaries like Spartacus or Catiline, but by men like Julius Caesar and Augustus, who made Roman militarism constructive and pacific instead of destructive and selfish. Western civilisation today is waiting for its Augustus; it needs consolidation rather than revolution, not, of course, in the sense of an Imperial unification by military power, but in the form of a social consolidation and a stabilising of economic conditions.

The foundation of the League of Nations proves at least that there is a general realisation of the need for world peace and international action for common ends. But it also shows how far these ideals are at present from practical realisation, and how deep is the inner disunity of our civilisation. There is not only an opposition of material interests and ambitions among the peoples of Europe, there are fundamental differences of mental outlook and ideals. Our culture has lost its unity, not only internationally, but morally, even within the limits of the individual societies of which Europe is composed.

And this brings us to a deeper problem than any of the three we have already discussed, for it is upon the moral and spiritual unity of a culture that its external life ultimately depends. For Europe is not, as we are often inclined to believe, a group of peoples held together by a common type of material culture; it is a spiritual society which owes its very existence to the religious tradition which for a thousand years moulded the beliefs, the ideals, and the institutions of the European peoples. Even the Reformation and the centuries of religious and international strife that followed it did not entirely destroy this common tradition. Europe remained Christendom, though it was a Christendom secularised and divided. The vision of its lost unity haunted the mind of Europe, and inspired the men of the eighteenth century with their enthusiasm for the abstract ideals of humanity and a new social order. They felt that Europe was being born again and that the union of humanity was at hand.

But the new age saw the frustration of all these hopes. The vast progress of material civilisation and of man's control over nature in the nineteenth century was not accompanied by the corresponding advance in spiritual unity.

It seemed as though the new powers had outstripped all social control, and that man was becoming the slave of the machinery that he had created. While the ancient Greeks, or the men of the Middle Ages, had used their poor resources to create great artistic works as the material embodiment of their social and spiritual ideals, the men of the nineteenth century used their vast powers to build up the ugly, unhealthy, and disorderly cities of the industrial era, which seem devoid of form or of any common social purpose.

It is true that there was no decline in the activity of intellectual life, but here also there was a complete absence of cultural unity; science, religion, philosophy, and literature each went on its way regardless of the others.

The mind of the age was divided against itself; it no longer possessed a common conception of reality capable of uniting the different activities of individual minds. This intellectual division and the consequent failure to achieve spiritual unity were the inevitable consequences of the spirit that had dominated European thought ever since the Reformation. They were in fact the price that modern culture had to pay for the conquest of nature and the immense progress of physical science.

For the downfall of the great medieval synthesis destroyed the inner unity of European thought. It was a victory for physical science, which was emancipated from the dead hand of the Aristotelian cosmology, and left free to enter into its new heritage. But it was a defeat for philosophy, which now lost its former undisputed intellectual hegemony, and became a wanderer and an outcast with no sure foothold in the world of reality. Like a discredited political leader, it was continually offering its services as a mediator between the opposing parties, only to be disavowed by both sides and left to bear the responsibility for their blunders.

From the seventeenth century onwards the modern scientific movement has been based on the mechanistic view of nature which regards the world as a closed material order moved by purely mechanical and mathematical laws. All the aspects of reality which could not be reduced to mathematical terms and regarded as resulting from the blind operation of material forces were treated as mere subjective impressions of the human mind, and since man himself was viewed as a by-product of this vast mechanical order, they were inevitably deprived of any ultimate reality.

A universe of this kind seems to leave no room for moral values or spiritual forces; indeed, it is hard to see what place the mind of the scientific observer himself has in the blind and endless flux of configurations of atoms which is the substance of reality. This was pointed out forcibly enough by philosophic critics, but their arguments fell on deaf ears; whatever theoretic objections could be brought against the mechanistic hypothesis, it was undeniably successful as a basis for scientific research, and consequently it was accepted without further question as an established truth. As Professor Whitehead has said, "While the Middle Ages were an age of faith based upon reason, the eighteenth century was an age of reason based upon faith" — i.e., on the unreasoning acceptance of the mechanistic hypothesis.

The physicists lost all interest in metaphysics, and renounced the attempt to solve the ultimate problems of being, while the philosophers for their part turned away from physical reality to an ideal world which had its only existence in the human mind. A great deal has been written, especially during the nineteenth century, on the conflict of religion and science, but the opposition of science and philosophy was actually more fundamental. As a matter of fact, a large number, perhaps the majority, of the greatest scientists have been profoundly religious and orthodox Christians like Volta and Cauchy, Dalton and Faraday, Pasteur and Mendel, and Wallace; hardly one of them since the eighteenth century has been a philosopher. For, strange though it may appear, a faith in the mechanistic hypothesis is far more easily reconcilable with a belief in theological dogmas than with any kind of metaphysical system.[59]

On the other hand, nineteenth-century philosophy, by turning in the direction of absolute idealism, had lost all contact with the world of science. Hegel's *Philosophy of Nature* is far more widely removed from contemporary scientific thought than are the systems of Plato and Aristotle.[60] To quote Professor Whitehead again: "The history of thought in the eighteenth and nineteenth centuries is governed by the fact that the world had got hold of a general idea which it could neither live with nor live without." Scientific materialism introduces order into the world of natural phenomena which had so long defied all attempts at rationalization; but at the same time it produces anarchy in the moral and spiritual order. Thus it bore fruit in the nineteenth-century individualizing of morals; for, as Professor Whitehead points out, the reduction of non-material values to subjective impressions, or even the Cartesian doctrine of minds as separate substance, "leads directly, not

---

[59] It is true that Comte aimed at creating a philosophy, which should be thoroughly scientific, but to do this he had not only to abandon all metaphysics, but to attempt the purging of science itself of its theoretical and abstract elements and its limitations to strictly practical and "positive" objects. Thus all he actually achieved was the synthesis of a partial aspect of science with an even more limited type of religion.

[60] Cf. E. Meyerson, *De l'Explication dans les Sciences*, vol. ii., for an interesting criticism of the Hegelian attitude to natural science.

merely to private worlds of experience, but also to private worlds of morals." "Also the assumption of the bare valuelessness of mere matter led to a lack of reverence in the treatment of natural or artistic beauty."[61] And in the realm of...... economics and sociology the consequences were no less disastrous. The nineteenth-century economists, such as Ricardo and James Mill, conceived economic laws on the analogy of the mechanical laws of physical science, thus excluding all moral factors and preparing the way for the Marxian "materialist interpretation of history," which represents the complete application of mechanistic ideas to social phenomena.

In biology Darwin himself was influenced both by the physicists and the economists in his central doctrine of the evolution of species through the pressure of population on food supply and the consequent struggle for existence in which only the fittest survived. But a world that is the product of chance and the blind working of material forces leaves no room for the golden hopes for the future of humanity which had been so characteristic of the eighteenth-century creed. Even social reform and humanitarian ideals seemed difficult to reconcile with the mechanical view of social evolution, and the theory of the survival of the fittest was popularly interpreted in the crudely selfish form that used to be known to the French as "*le struggle for life-isme.*" Today all that is changed. There is a reaction all along the line against the old scientific materialism, whether in

---

[61] Whitehead, *Science and the Modern World*, p. 281.

physics, biology, or sociology, and the mathematicians and physicists themselves are abandoning the old mechanistic hypothesis in favour of new and wider conceptions of reality.

This change is to some extent due to the theory of Relativity and to Einstein's criticism of the Newtonian physics, but it is not confined to Einsteinian circles. It is now almost universally admitted that science cannot pretend to give an exhaustive causal explanation of reality, but is merely a translation of reality into mathematical symbols or imagery. Scientific laws have a somewhat similar relation to nature as the printed musical score has to the sound of one of Beethoven's sonatas, or, as Professor Eddington has said, they have as much resemblance to the real qualities of Nature as a telephone number has to a subscriber. Thus the aspects of reality that are revealed in religion, philosophy, and art may be no less true and no less ultimate than the knowledge that is derived from physical science. Only their method of approach is different; for they conceive reality in terms of substance, quality, and value, whereas science views the world exclusively in terms of quantitative relations. Hence the representatives of the most advanced school of scientific thought, like Professor Whitehead or Professor Eddington, are entirely at one with the adherents of the scholastic and theological tradition such as Jacques Maritain in their criticism of the mechanistic theory of nature and their demand for a return to the eternal spiritual values. Thus the intellectual schism between scientific knowledge and moral and spiritual values, which has introduced so much division and anarchy into European culture, seems no longer inevitable, and conditions seem favourable to a return of Western civilisation to spiritual unity. Europe today stands in the same need of moral and social reconstruction as did the Mediterranean world in the first century B.C.

The Augustan movement attempted to solve the problem by the restoration of the traditional religious foundations on which the political and family life of the Roman State rested, and in spite of the impossibility of a real return to the peasant simplicity of the Religion of Numa, the effect was not wholly unsuccessful, for it inspired the highest spiritual expression of the Latin genius. After the arid Puritanism of Cato and the scientific pessimism of Lucretius there comes the profoundly spiritual and catholic genius of Virgil, which expressed itself in one of the greatest religious poems of the world.

It is a mistake to regard the religious policy of Augustus as a mere piece of political expediency. If his attempt was ultimately a failure, that was due more to the intrinsic poverty of the tradition which it sought to restore rather than to any lack of moral earnestness.

The task of modern Europe is at once more complicated and more hopeful. We possess an incomparably richer spiritual heritage than that of the Roman culture. The Roman world-empire was an artificial unity with no common cultural tradition behind it, whereas modern civilisation is built on the foundations of an age-long community of religion and intellectual culture.

The two essential elements that have gone to the making of European culture are the Christian religion and the scientific tradition. To the former it owes its moral unity and its belief in its world mission, while the latter has given it its power of material organisation and its control over nature. Without religion, science becomes a neutral force which lends itself to the service of militarism and economic exploitation as readily as to the service of humanity. Without science, on the other hand, society becomes fixed in an immobile, unprogressive order like that of the great Oriental civilisations or the Byzantine culture. It is only by the co-operation of both these forces that European civilisation can succeed in reaching the goal that it has set before itself during the last two centuries. The reconciliation of religion and science is the function of philosophy which has been temporarily thrust out of its proper kingdom by the victory of the mechanistic world view.

The specifically Western ideals that found their expression in the Liberalism and Humanitarianism of the eighteenth and nineteenth centuries have temporarily broken down, because they were based on a superficial synthesis which only succeeded in uniting the etiolated ghost of the Christian tradition with the phantasm of a pseudo-scientific rationalism. Consequently it was rejected alike by the most living religion and by the most genuine scientific thought of the new age. Nevertheless, the central idea that inspired the movement—the belief in the possibility of a new world order based on justice and fraternal charity—is as living as ever, and waits only for a new intellectual foundation to become a constructive force in the world today. The present crisis is due as much to an excess of misdirected idealism as to the destructive forces of class hatred and international strife, and if the former is once more directed towards positive ends, there is no reason to doubt the possibility of a further great development of European culture. After the age of civil war and military exploitation came the centuries of the Roman peace, and the strife and discords of the transitional period of modern Europe may also be the prelude to an age of world civilisation under Western leadership.

Christopher Dawson, 1927

www.ingramcontent.com/pod-product-compliance
Lightning Source LLC
Chambersburg PA
CBHW020932180426
43192CB00036B/892